You Can't Take It With You:

The Art and Science of Legacy Fundraising

Fraser Green
Holly Wagg
Charlotte Field

You Can't Take It With You:
The Art and Science of Legacy Fundraising

ISBN-10: 978-1091190504
Front cover design and layout by Sean Mercer.
Book design and layout by Alison Turmelle.

Manufactured by Kindle Direct Publishing.

Published in Canada by:
Good Works Communications Inc.
110-1101 Prince of Wales Drive
Ottawa, ON K2C 3W7

CONTENTS

Where Did the Title Come From?   i

Foreword   iii

PROLOGUE: ix
Meet Jacqueline

CHAPTER 1:   1
Today's Legacy Landscape

CHAPTER 2:   9
Identifying Your Legacy Donor

CHAPTER 3:   27
Raindrops on the Roof: Timing Your Legacy
Marketing

CHAPTER 4:   35
Crafting Your Legacy Strategy and Guiding
Principles

CHAPTER 5:   47
The Giving Brain

CHAPTER 6:   73
Storytelling for a Legacy Audience

CHAPTER 7:   93
The Legacy Factory: Tactics and Tools

CHAPTER 8:   127
Stewardship and Recognition of Expectancies

CHAPTER 9:   141
How to Model Your Legacy ROI

CHAPTER 10:   153
Making Legacy Giving an Office Priority

CHAPTER 11:   163
Final Thoughts

References   168

About the Authors   172

About Good Works   174

WHERE DID THE TITLE COME FROM?

The title of this book comes straight from an interview with a legacy donor.

Before we write their stories, we like to learn everything we can about these most incredible individuals. It's such a privilege for someone to share their life story with you. During these conversations, we explore everything from their birth to their childhood to pivotal moments in their lives that have shaped the human being they've become today.

When it came time to ask that all-important question – *"What made you want to leave a gift in your will?"* – this particular donor supplied an answer that we'd never heard before.

She cleared her throat. Laughed a little in spite of herself. And then said, *"Have you ever seen a U-Haul following a hearse? You can't take it with you!"*

Did you just take a sip of your water and spit it out? We most certainly did!

We're not sure about the origin of this expression. It could be something we attribute to our wonderful donor, but we've also read that credit should go to Denzel Washington in a 2011 graduation speech.

Those six words are the perfect summary of what we hope you take from this book. You have no use for your assets when you die. But, you can put those assets to work to build a well that draws up clean water, or build a new shelter to house abandoned cats, or buy an MRI machine for your local community hospital, or to fund research that will change the face of personalized cancer treatment.

You can't take it with you. But you can still change the world.

-    Fraser, Holly, and Charlotte

FOREWORD

Think for a minute about the gift you're most proud of. The one you worked on that may not be the biggest amount of money, or the one that got the press treatment, but it was about you and a donor creating a gift that cut to the core of your charity's cause and spoke to the soul of why that donor gives. It was magic right?

We are living in an exciting time where Canada is realizing we can't leave philanthropy up to philanthropists. The data tells us that everyday donors are the ones who move the needle to affect the causes most vital to the health of our society and the world.

This book is going to help you create more gifts like that.

A decade ago the groundbreaking book *Iceberg Philanthropy: Unlocking Extraordinary Gifts from Ordinary Donors* was ahead of its time. It outlined the looming demographic shift that would propel planned giving from the top of the theoretical donor pyramid onto the desks and into the job descriptions of all fundraisers. I was the book's biggest fan and have pestered Fraser and his team for a sequel. And we've never needed it more.

Today, the iceberg has melted and the largest wealth transfer in modern history is happening. A vast amount of assets are in play and if we don't help every charity to access the tidal wave of giving that this asset transfer is creating, they will lose out.

It's well known that early adopters often sound like zealots. I must admit that Fraser Green and the team at Good Works for many years, made me uncomfortable. No that's too polite… they downright freaked me out.

When I joined the fundraising community in the late 1990s, the focus was on special events and the gold rush of annual giving fueled by the fact that cash was king. The small but growing major gift community was suiting up and studying moves management, the medium was paper, and charities didn't have websites. Planned giving had been around for decades but its narrative was deferred giving and most education focused on the idea that the math was the message. That 1 Donor + 1 Cause x Giving Vehicles would = Gifts.

But Good Works preached the connection between charity and donor fuelled by uncomfortable ideas like passion and love (could we talk about love in our direct mail letters?). Their take was rooted in demographic research and hard data from hundreds of campaigns. All the other books and main voices in planned giving at the time were written by professorial purveyors of tools and tactics.

But Fraser kept talking about feelings and the profiles of donors. Why the unrelenting focus on the human being at the root of philanthropy? Because Good Works knew then what the fundraising sector has finally caught up to – heart beats head – but you need both. The 'how' is not enough, you NEED a 'why'.

The world has changed since *Iceberg Philanthropy* was written. Not only has the world gone digital, we have moved past the homepage of your website and even social media is over a decade old. Engagement has shifted the donor acquisition process into the devices that shape how we live and how we give.

As the Civic generation gives way to the Baby Boomers, the majority of major and planned givers now have to acquire a whole new set of emotionally intelligent skills and asset-based strategies which inform how we talk about doing good. Hard and soft skills have switched places. Add to that the reality that there is a pervasive culture in charity of doing more with less. The pendulum has swung back to integrated teams doing everything which means when it comes to deferred giving, there's been time for nothing.

I wasn't sure they could pull this book off. But boy, did they deliver and then some!

Good Works as a team has evolved to include Holly and Charlotte, and a whole boatload of other talented fundraisers. They are the next generation of leaders who have the skills to integrate digital tools into time-tested marketing. And, since this group of professionals are deeply engaged with hundreds of charity teams of all sizes, they wrote from what they know. The real lives and capacity of today's fundraiser and the challenges charities face.

You are going to see yourself in this book.

Also, this is a team whose core value is positivity and hope, who have personally faced challenges that charities face on a daily basis. I can't express how moving it was for me, and I hope it will be for you too, to read the real talk about how hard it is to be a fundraiser today. They'll affirm that you do need to have a strategy to win the office wars and fight for your budget, despite the fact that planned giving has lived on the side of your desk. We need all hands on deck today.

This is a triumphant resource that will cause you to think. It will give you the secrets of strategy so you have the confidence to act and the tools to do it, in your shop, right away.

After two decades in planned giving myself, I've worked with charities both large and small, worked in a financial institution with Donor Advised Funds and Private Foundations and now as Vice President of the Canadian Association of Gift Planners, I wholeheartedly agree that it's time we face so many of the challenges that this book will address. The hard truths that pyramids and silos separate the strategy that the donor journey brings together. That data and demographics need to factor into history and personality because the ultimate gift is deeply personal and not generic. That even though tax, finance, and law can be cold, clean, sanitized administration, no gift will happen unless we as fundraisers put on hip waders and jump into the swamp of vulnerable uncertainty and have open-hearted donor discussions about giving, legacy, and purpose.

Thank you to Good Works for creating a roadmap to demystify planned giving with this book.

Dear reader, you are going to go on a journey to break down every roadblock and objection that has ever been thrown in front of a fundraiser that has sabotaged the success of integrating planned giving into fundraising. From the excuses we use in our charity that we don't have time for deferred gift discussions, the denial that cash is still king and assets are too complex a conversation. From the donor objections as to why they can't give and the emotional issues that trigger doubt in asset and estate giving. That we can't easily raise, track, count, and recognize planned gifts until our whole shop knows what they are and feel that they can be part of the process.

In these pages, you will find inspiration to deliver on the aspiration of so many charities — to successfully launch, grow, and sustain a planned giving program. And, you'll have a lot more fun and fulfilment in your work as a fundraiser because we've all been overthinking this. You're going to reconnect with why we do this work.

Remember that gift you were most proud of? What about that donor? Think about them as you finish each chapter of this book and think about how what you're learning is going to empower you to help more awesome donors to paint a future of hope, possibility, accessibility, justice, equality, and progress using the strategy and skills you are learning. Together, you will engage their passion and your charity's purpose to result in a powerful, beautiful, legacy of philanthropy.

Sure, they can't take it with them. But you're going to learn how to help your donors amplify their impact, to do more good and change the world.

Paul C. Nazareth
19 Year Planned Giving Educator

PROLOGUE:
MEET JACQUELINE

Jacqueline Barbour was born in Selkirk, Manitoba in June of 1947. Her father, who grew up in a farming family in the area, had just returned from service in WW2, and Jacqueline would turn out to be the eldest of six children in the family. Jacqueline's mother was a farm wife and mother. She was simple and frugal and deeply dedicated to family, church, and community.

Jacqueline was a very good student and loved to read. She was also quite musical – playing piano and singing whenever and wherever she got the chance. As a young girl, Jacqueline didn't particularly stand out. She was well liked by everyone, but not the most popular girl in her class. She liked sports but didn't really excel. While she enjoyed the company of friends, Jacqueline loved to spend time alone with her books, her dad's records, or the family piano.

Jacqueline aspired to pursue higher education, but when she graduated high school in 1965, there weren't all that many options available to young women. Most professions, like law, medicine, business, and engineering were all very much male-dominated. Nursing and teaching were the two 'women's professions' that required a higher education back then. Jacqueline chose teaching.

She left Selkirk to attend Winnipeg Teachers' College for a year and earned her Manitoba teaching certificate. When she graduated, she saw an opening for a Grade 2 teacher in Brandon, Manitoba. She applied for the job, got it, and the next August she moved to Brandon to start her adult life.

Jacqueline loved teaching. She adored her kids and they adored her right back. Jacqueline was able to infect her students with her love of reading – and soon her 7-year-olds were lost in stories from around the world. It was a magical time for Jacqueline. She had found her calling.

During her second year of teaching, she met a young man named Wilf Hassell at a church social event. Wilf was a Brandon native and, after earning a business degree at the University of Manitoba, had returned home to become the Assistant Manager of the local branch of the Royal Bank.

A courtship began – and on June 27, 1968, Jacqueline and Wilf were married at St. Luke's Anglican Church in Brandon. (Two days before their wedding, Canadians had elected Pierre Elliott Trudeau as Canada's 15th Prime Minister. Four days after their wedding, Medicare came into effect in Canada, affording publicly-funded healthcare services to all Canadians).

After a one-week honeymoon in Vancouver (neither of them had ever ventured outside Manitoba before), they returned to Brandon. Wilf returned to the bank and Jacqueline began looking for a house for them to settle in. She found a charming newer split-level house in the Valleyview neighbourhood of Brandon and they bought it despite its whopping $22,500 price tag. They assumed a $17,000 mortgage amortized over 25 years. They were both uncomfortable with the massive debt they had just undertaken.

By Christmas of 1968, Jacqueline was pregnant with their first child. In June of 1969 she had a baby girl that they named Brenda. Somewhat reluctantly, Jacqueline resigned from her teaching position with the Brandon & District School Board and dedicated herself to her home and family for the foreseeable future. Two more children soon followed: Sharon in 1971 and Michael in 1973. The Hassells were now a full-fledged family living a comfortable middle-class life in a small Canadian city.

With Michael's birth, Jacqueline and Wilf decided it was high time to make their wills. They visited a lawyer in town and had him draw up simple wills that made each spouse the sole beneficiary of the other's estate. The kids would become beneficiaries should their parents die together.

Jacqueline was a devoted mother who, for the most part at least, loved dedicating herself to her family. She volunteered to help with class trips and was constantly chauffeuring the kids to dance lessons, hockey practices, and Girl Guide and Boy Scout meetings. She was an active fixture at St. Luke's, where the family attended service and Sunday school every week, and Jacqueline sang in the choir and served on the outreach and stewardship committee.

Both Jacqueline and Wilf felt strongly that it was their duty to teach their kids to be grateful, thoughtful, and generous. Every Christmas, the family would volunteer to help support poor families in town. The kids were encouraged and rewarded by their mom and dad for anything they initiated that benefited the less fortunate in some way.

Jacqueline and Wilf made time for themselves every week. They golfed when the weather allowed and they curled in the wintertime. Jacqueline stayed in touch with her brothers and sisters and there were annual road trips to the various family homes and cottages to ensure that all the cousins stayed close and connected. In 1977, the Hassells bought a piece of land on Lake Wahtopanah. Over the next three years, they and the kids built a cottage that would become their summer retreat for the next 40 years.

As the kids grew older (and could get themselves to dance and hockey practice), Jacqueline was eager to re-engage with the outside world. She had been following the 'women's lib movement' and was energized by the idea of gender equality. She returned to supply teaching on a part-time basis, she canvassed her neighbourhood to raise funds for the Canadian Cancer Society every spring, and she began volunteering in the new palliative care centre at the Brandon Hospital.

When she was in her late 40s, Jacqueline discovered a lump on her breast. In consultation with her doctor, she decided to have it removed just to be safe. Two years later, her sister Gail was diagnosed with breast cancer and lost her battle within the year. These events triggered a deep commitment in Jacqueline to do whatever she could to contribute to the fight against the disease. In 1992, she ran in the Canadian Cancer Society's 'Relay for Life' event, and continued to run in the event for a decade. She later became a monthly donor to the Canadian Cancer Society as well.

By the late 1990s, the kids were all educated and starting families of their own. Jacqueline and Wilf became doting grandparents, travelling to visit grandkids in Winnipeg, Calgary, and Saskatoon whenever they could. They stayed physically active and remained very involved in the community. In their own unassuming way, Jacqueline and Wilf had become true pillars of their town.

It was around this time that they decided to update their wills for the first time. They added their grandkids as beneficiaries, and they also decided to leave a gift to the Canadian Cancer Society, in part to honour Jacqueline's late sister. The gift was 5% of their estate, which didn't seem like much, but at least it was a little something.

Wilf retired from the bank in 2010 and he and Jacqueline bought a timeshare in Phoenix, Arizona where they would spend part of their winters. After four decades of marriage, they had reached a truly happy and contented place in their lives. The hard work and struggles were pretty much behind them. They had their health and good energy. Their kids had turned out well. The house was paid for and their retirement years were financially secure. Wilf and Jacqueline enjoyed their days – and each other's company – very much. They counted their blessings and looked forward to a joyful and relaxed future.

After five years of retirement, Wilf was diagnosed with pancreatic cancer. All of a sudden, their happy, secure life was shattered. Wilf bravely went through the radiation and chemo, but to no avail. Despite the best efforts of the medical staff at the Brandon Hospital, he died in the spring of 2016.

After Wilf's passing, Jacqueline found herself taking over sole responsibility for her finances. Being a bank manager by trade, Wilf had always assumed responsibility for managing the family's money – and he did it well. As Jacqueline began managing the money, she also realized that she needed to update her will, once again. She ensured that her three kids and five grandkids got equal shares of 10% of her estate. And she now allotted 10% shares to two charities: the Canadian Cancer Society and the Brandon Hospital Foundation, in recognition of the superb care they had provided to Wilf during his last months.

Today, Jacqueline is older and moves a little slower. But, she still lives a busy life with her church, community, golf, and curling. And, of course, her grandchildren. She stays in touch with her siblings, nieces, and nephews via Facebook and email. She still misses Wilf terribly, but she's found contentment.

These days, Jacqueline has the opportunity and the inclination to look back and reflect on her life. She's proud of what she's done with her journey. She's taught hundreds of wonderful children. She's raised her own kids to be strong, independent, kind, and generous adults. She shared a great love with a wonderful man for more than 40 years. She's given back to her community and maintained the faith that is so central to her life.

When she thinks of the legacy she'll leave behind, she thinks first of her children, and then her grandchildren. But then she thinks about her friends, her neighbours, her community, and her world. She feels a deep sense of satisfaction knowing that those gifts in her will to cancer research and her community hospital will each amount to a little over $100,000 when she's gone. It amazes her to think that the house they bought so long ago is now worth more than $400,000 – and that her total net worth is in excess of a million dollars.

Jacqueline knows deep down that her journey has been a wonderful one.

- She has always lived with purpose and meaning. She has always had important work to do that mattered to herself and others.

- She has always felt a deep sense of belonging – to her immediate family, to her church, to her community, and to her fellow humans in general. Jacqueline has never felt isolated or alone, even after Wilf died.

- And, most importantly, Jacqueline has always given and received a lot of love freely. As she reflects and prays now, she appreciates more than ever the gift of love and time with loved ones that she has been given.

When Jacqueline passes on from this life, she will leave her love behind. It will transcend her in her children and in her children's children. She has left small touches of love with the thousands of people whose lives have intersected with hers. And, she has sent her love into the future to people she will never meet with the bequests she has made in her will.

Jacqueline doesn't know how much time she has left in this life. But, she's happy to accept each day as it comes, and live it to the fullest.

She is content.

She is at peace.

She has lived a good life.

CHAPTER 1:
TODAY'S LEGACY LANDSCAPE

So, we've just met Jacqueline, and we've seen where a gift in her will fits in the overall story arc of her life. Jacqueline is representative of the literally millions of donors out there over the age of 60 – many of whom are going to make legacy gifts to charity.

Now, what does this mean to you as a fundraiser? How can you tap into all those Jacquelines out there and communicate with them in a way that's going to persuade them to make a bequest to you?

Before we get into the '*here's how you do it*' meat of the book (and we'll get there, we promise!), we want to place legacy giving into its larger context. Any strategist worth their salt knows that a deep understanding of the landscape is critical to mapping the best route to your desired destination.

So let's take a few pages to look at the big picture...

We've got good news and bad news for you. Let's start with the bad news:

The world is a busier place than it's ever been before. Your life is busier than it's ever been before. We have more education. More information. More entertainment options. More ways to do things faster, cheaper, more efficiently...

There was a time not that long ago when a Caribbean vacation meant a decent hotel, an all-you-can-eat restaurant, a pool, and a beach. Everyone went for their winter holidays pretty much looking for the same thing — lots of sun, lots of sand, lots of water, and probably free adult beverages to boot.

Today, you might be on the hunt for a secluded beachfront resort with no more than 60 rooms. You want a yoga experience, complete with three classes a day, guided and independent meditation time slots, and on-site yogi gurus who will give you one-on-one coaching if you need it. And of course, you might want Egyptian cotton sheets with a 900+ thread count, Ayurvedic healing seminars, and macrobiotic vegan food.

In other words, in a single generation, products and services have fractured and splintered all over the place. And charitable giving is no exception: Back in the 1980s and early 1990s, most charities had a donor base and a direct mail program. And that was pretty much it. Okay, maybe they ran a special event or two, and the more sophisticated charities did some major gift work, but fundraising was a pretty simple process. Send your mail. Count your money. Send more mail.

How times have changed!

There have been two big shifts in the philanthropic marketplace since the good old days of the 80s and 90s.

THE DIGITAL REVOLUTION

Technology has transformed the way we communicate. It has changed how we learn, how we work, how we shop, how we have fun – and yes, how we give!

Communications expert Bernard Gauthier likes to talk about the speeding parade. He likens communications to a parade. There are floats and bands and clowns – just like the parades you take your kids to.

A generation ago, parades were simple affairs. You stood on the sidewalk and watched as a couple of dozen floats crawled by. The bands and clowns walked past you in a pretty leisurely fashion.

Today, the floats and bands are whizzing by at 160 kilometres an hour. They're a blur. And there are 4,000 floats in today's parade. Four thousand floats at 160 kilometres an hour. How in the world do you keep track? You don't.

Worse yet, look at this parade from another vantage point.

You and your friends have decided to enter a float in the parade. You're hoping to win first prize as the "Best New Float" in this year's event. After the parade, the audience will vote to select the winner. Yet this parade is huge and it's terribly fast. How will the crowd even *notice* your float let alone pick it as their favourite?

The float is your charity. The audience is your pool of donors and prospects. The other floats are your competition. The parade is a day in the life of your donor.

Instead of just sending four or five direct mail appeals a year (and counting the money!), charities are now running an email solicitation/stewardship stream, they're on the street asking for monthly gifts, they have social media strategies, mid-level, leadership, and major gift programs, and all sorts of special events. They may also have corporate sponsors, a cause marketing effort, crowdfunding, and peer-to-peer fundraising.

There are literally dozens of best practice fundraising tactics available to charities today. The hard part is picking the few that have the best potential to grow your revenues effectively, efficiently, and predictably. (We think we have one for you – read on!)

MORE COMPETITION

Since the mid-1990s, we've experienced a new intensity of fierce competition for donor dollars. There have been two primary drivers for this increased competitiveness, in our opinion.

First, back in the mid-1990s, charities in Canada fundraised to the tune of about $6 billion dollars per year. Back then, Canada had a Finance Minister named Paul Martin who set about to put the federal government's fiscal house in order. He successfully tackled Canada's deficit and debt problems – but at a price. During his tenure as Minister of Finance (1993 to 2002), government funding to the charitable sector (particularly health and education) was cut by some $15 billion.

All across the country, hospitals, health charities, universities and colleges, international development NGOs, and social service agencies reeled under these cuts. Boards of directors had painful discussions about falling revenue. And, as a result, fundraising directors were told to '*go find more money.*' Now, this was all well and good, but there wasn't necessarily any more money to be found.

Next, thanks to an over-extended mortgage market in the USA, we had a financial meltdown in 2008, the likes of which the developed world had not seen since the Great Depression of the 1930s. Fortunes crumbled. Savings were lost. Jobs were cut. Gloom grew. And, of course, giving was depressed as people felt less confident of their own financial self-sufficiency.

Despite the objective evidence that there was less philanthropic money to be had, boards of directors still told fundraisers to get out there and '*find more.*' Our sector was changed in that the new practice was to expect fundraisers to '*do more with less.*' Fundraising became a more difficult, pressure-packed, and demanding profession than it ever had been before.

Even though the meltdown of 2008 is history today, its legacy is still firmly embedded in the practice of fund development. We are under what seems to be permanent pressure to raise more with less.

So, that's the bad news – or at least some of it.

BUT THINGS ARE LOOKING UP

Now let's look for something that we fundraisers can be genuinely optimistic about!

Alongside the knowledge that fundraising tactics are fracturing, we can also segment audiences and target specific groups like never before. Back in the 1990s, we didn't hear many fundraisers talking about generational cohorts as distinct audiences. Yet today, everyone you listen to has a new 'Millennial Strategy' that will raise you tons of money. We're big believers that generational cohorts generally have their own distinct values, beliefs, attitudes, and behaviours. And, of the four cohorts that fundraisers talk about – Civics (born pre-1946), Baby Boomers (1946-1966), Gen Xers (1967-1982), and Millennials (post-1982) – we are going to focus this book on the two older generations.

We know from Statistics Canada and the Canada Revenue Agency how much charitable money is donated each year. But beyond that, Good Works research has shown the landslide of money that's on its way over the next generation.

Based on our most recent (2019) market research in partnership with Environics, we can project that more than 1.5 million living Canadians have already made bequests with a total value of about $216 billion. That's right – $216 billion – compared to total charitable giving this year which will be less than $10 billion.

AND HERE WE ARE TODAY

Back in 2007, we wrote a book called *Iceberg Philanthropy*. At the time, we felt like Christopher Columbus telling Queen Isabella *"I'm PRETTY sure the earth is round!"* Back then, we had a radical idea.

Our hypothesis was pretty much as follows: Icebergs, when viewed from above the water's surface, are only 10% visible to the human eye. That means 90% or more of the actual ice is hidden from view below the waterline. It's the same with charitable bequests. Average middle-class Canadians are making bequests to charities, not from their annual income, but from the accrued value of their paid-off homes and retirement savings. There are millions of middle-class Canadians who are open to your invitation to consider making a gift in their will to your charity. If you employ a <u>steady,</u> consistent <u>drip marketing strategy over many years</u>, you will access millions of dollars from these quiet, unassuming donors.

There are several Canadian charities who decided to try the strategy we outlined in *Iceberg Philanthropy* as early adopters, and their risk-taking has paid big dividends. We know of many charities who market bequests in an ongoing manner and who are earning planned giving revenue they wouldn't have dreamed of 20 years ago. The peaks in their legacy revenue correlate to the years that they ran legacy marketing programs with us.

In essence, back in 2007 we felt that we had to persuade you that you should be trying to raise more money from bequests – because it was the largely untapped frontier of new philanthropic revenue. We talked a little about the need to have a strategic marketing program. And we didn't talk much at all about how to actually do this work.

Good Workers have been very busy in the years since then. We've been doing legacy communications and campaigning non-stop with well over a hundred Canadian charities of all shapes and sizes. We've made some goofy mistakes, and had some spectacular wins. We've honed our craft to the point where we feel we have earned our reputation as the best legacy gift storytellers.

With this book, it's different. We're assuming that you already know that there's lots of legacy money to be earned out there. We're pretty much assuming that you know you need to have a consistent legacy gift marketing plan.

This time, we're going to spend a lot more time showing you who to talk to, what to say, what channels to use, how to project costs and revenues, and what pitfalls you might expect along the way.

Ultimately, our original hypothesis has proven true. There are literally millions of everyday Canadians who are making their life's most extraordinary gifts through their wills — funded by the value of their paid-off homes. And, there are many more of these gifts to be made and realized in the years to come.

So, what are you waiting for? Read on, and discover what could very well be the most amazing and transcending philanthropic journey of your life. We promise on our mothers' souls that you'll enjoy the ride!

CHAPTER 2:
IDENTIFYING YOUR LEGACY DONOR

There's an age-old saying in the direct mail fundraising world that goes like this: '*Who you mail to is more important than what you mail.*' In our 30 years in direct response fundraising, we have found this idea to be pretty much true.

When it comes to marketing legacy gifts, choosing your audience is the absolute critical first step. If you take shortcuts here, you will compromise your ultimate revenue results for years, even decades, to come.

So, in this chapter, we'll give you a complete lay of the land on who your legacy donor really is. We'll start with a 40,000 foot view, and by the end of the chapter when we bring you in for landing, you'll have a complete profile of your ideal prospect who is living their life with their feet firmly planted on this earth.

THE STATE OF THE LEGACY NATION

You might have read our whitepaper, *The State of the Legacy Nation*. It's our take on a quantitative and thoughtful review of the entire legacy market, based on polling data from 1,500 Canadians. We first put it out in 2010, and then again in 2014 – and again in 2019, to give you the most up-to-date data possible.

This year's research polled English-speaking donors only. We learned in 2010 that Francophones are much less likely to leave bequests – and by focusing on English-speaking donors, we were able to get more accurate breakdowns by demographic segments (like income, region, and age).

We also added a new dimension that we'd been conjecturing about for years: we asked respondents to share their direct mail giving behaviour as well as their will-making and charitable bequesting. This allowed us to overlay results and examine direct mail donors as a distinct legacy audience in Canadian philanthropy.

Ultimately, we wanted to do our best to answer five key questions:

1. Who makes wills?
2. Who's going to make wills?
3. Who's making charitable bequests?
4. Who gets the money?
5. Where does all that money come from?

Here's what we learned, at a high level:

- Just over 1.5 million English-speaking Canadians alive today have made bequests to charities – up from 1.2 million in 2014.

- These donors have left about $216 billion to charity in their wills – up from $165 billion in 2014. (It's helpful to keep in mind that total receipted charitable giving in Canada is about $9.6 billion annually. The legacy money in Canadian wills today is the equivalent of 22.5 years' worth of annual Canadian giving!)

- The two big "sweet spots" for identifying your legacy prospects continue to be older donors and those who give to charity through the mail.

- The vast majority of the wealth in this huge market is found in the real estate that older middle-class people own. More specifically, it comes from homeowners who have paid off their mortgages and own their homes outright.

Question 1: Who Makes Wills?

Naturally, we wanted to start our research by finding out which Canadians have made wills – and what distinguishes those who have made wills from those who haven't. Here's what we found when we asked adults aged 18+ if they had made a will.

Overall, 42% of the surveyed adult English-speaking population currently has a will.

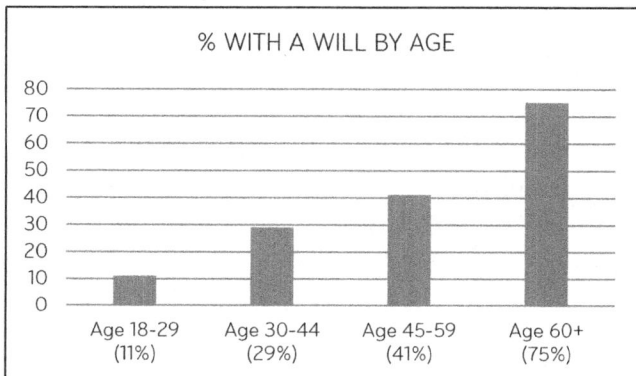

% WITH A WILL BY AGE

| | Age 18-29 (11%) | Age 30-44 (29%) | Age 45-59 (41%) | Age 60+ (75%) |

% WITH A WILL BY EDUCATION

| | High School Diploma or Less (32%) | College/University (45%) | Post-Graduate (47%) |

% WITH A WILL BY HOUSEHOLD INCOME

| <$30k (24%) | $30k-$50k (39%) | $50k-$80k (46%) | $80k-$100k (39%) | $100k+ (46%) |

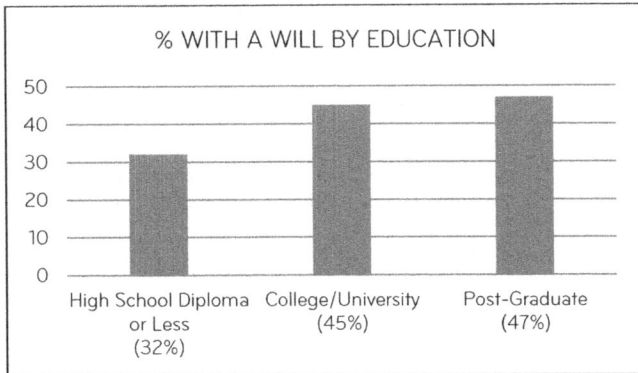

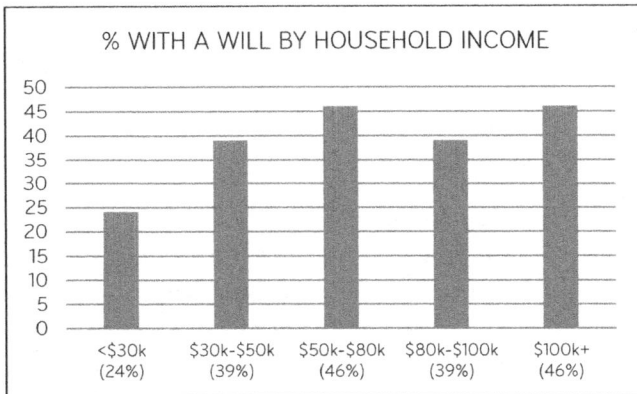

Our research showed that while geographic region and gender are not differentiating factors in will-making, employment status is. Fully 87% of the retired cohort have wills, while only 38% of full-time workers and only 22% of part-time workers do.

And, as we suspected, giving behaviour is also a key signifier in will-making. For the first time, we're able to confidently say that direct mail donors (51%) are significantly more likely to have a will than those who do not give to charity through the mail (35%). To take it a step further, about 80% of direct mail donors who make more than 10 direct mail gifts per year to charity have made wills.

Question 2: Who's Going To Make Wills?

More than half of English-speaking Canadian adults haven't yet made wills. This represents 12.5 million adults in Canada. We asked this group how likely they were to make a will within the next five year time frame.

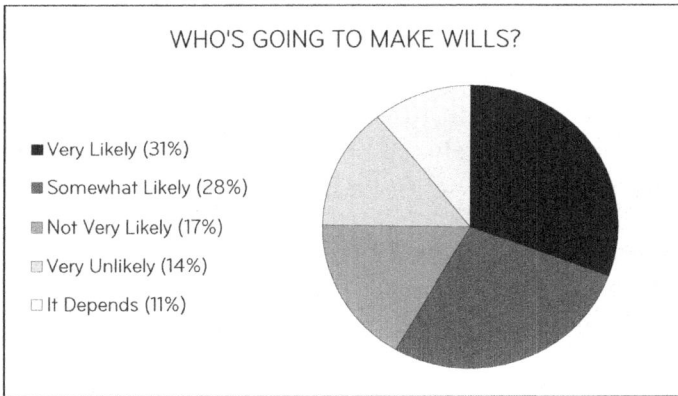

WHO'S GOING TO MAKE WILLS?

■ Very Likely (31%)
■ Somewhat Likely (28%)
▨ Not Very Likely (17%)
▢ Very Unlikely (14%)
☐ It Depends (11%)

The "very likely" candidates to be making wills in the next five years were disproportionately women, retired people, and people aged 60+.

When we do the math, there are more than 7 million Canadians who are either very likely or somewhat likely to make their wills in the next five years. Even if we were to assume that only a quarter of these people actually do make their wills, we would have 1.8 million Canadians with wills by 2024. This is a segment worth paying attention to!

Question 3: Who's Making Charitable Bequests?

The big story here is that direct mail donors stand out as the charitable bequest all-stars. More than any other factor (like gender, age, education, employment, region etc.), direct mail giving is the single biggest predictor of a charitable bequest. Fully 30% of self-reported direct mail donors have made charitable bequests – as opposed to only 7% of non-direct mail donors. If your charity has a direct mail program, you now have empirical evidence that you should be actively marketing legacy gifts to your donors!

Those households with earnings of $100,000+ are twice as likely (25%) to make charitable bequests as households in the <$30,000 category (12%). Similarly, respondents with the most education (graduate studies) are three times as likely (34%) to make charitable bequests as those with a high school education (10%).

Question 4: Who Gets The Money?
Now, we get down to the heart of the matter – namely where the money's going.

We asked those respondents who have already made their wills who they have named as beneficiaries. Here's where the money is headed:

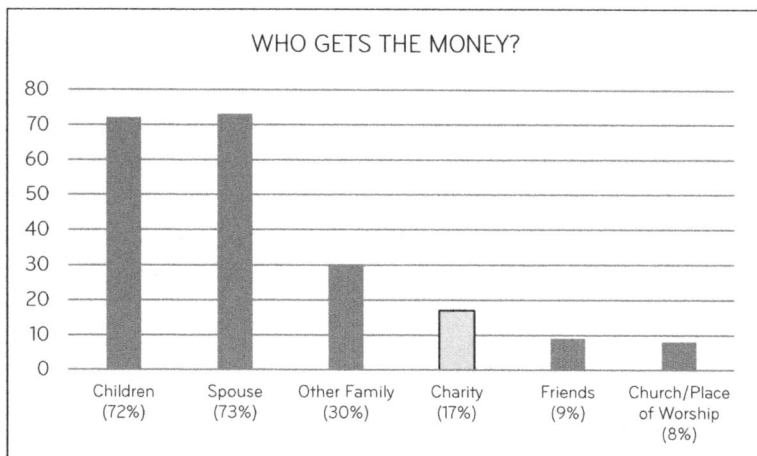

WHO GETS THE MONEY?

Children (72%), Spouse (73%), Other Family (30%), Charity (17%), Friends (9%), Church/Place of Worship (8%)

If we overlay the poll finding with Statistics Canada census data, we can estimate with confidence that more than 1.5 million English-speaking Canadians alive today have left bequests to charities in their wills.

(Note: While Statistics Canada and CRA group charity and church giving together, we believe that these are two distinct and different behaviours. That's why we separate charity and church giving when asking about beneficiaries.)

Question 5: Where Does All That Money Come From?

There are literally millions of Canadians who are living pretty everyday lives on pretty average incomes. Their lifestyles are modest, as is their philanthropy. They do alright, but they don't have money to burn by any means. These people, for the most part, are over the age of 60. Their kids, if they have kids, are educated and on their own. The people we're thinking about could either be in the last years of their careers, or partially or fully retired.

These everyday people (who are hiding in plain sight in your annual fund database) are sitting on a goldmine.

The 35 million people who live in Canada do so in about 14 million households. Of these households, 9.5 million – or 68% – are owner-occupied (as opposed to rented). Of these 9.5 million owner-occupied homes, a little over 3.9 million – or 41% – are mortgage-free.

Now we're getting at the goose who lays the golden legacy eggs. Let's determine the total value of those mortgage-free homes in Canada. The latest data available at the time of writing (in 2019) shows us that the average home price in Canada is almost bang on $500,000.

So, the total value of those paid-off homes is $1.95 trillion. We've been fundraisers for a long, long time – and this is the first time we've ever used the word 'trillion' in our work!

Finally, let's compare the estimated value of all legacy giving in Canada to the value of all those paid-for homes. The $216 billion we've estimated in legacy gifts is equivalent to 11% of the value of all those paid off mortgages.

Of course, we're not saying that every single legacy penny you'll receive over the next 20 years is going to come from middle-class homeowners. But we truly believe that the lion's share will. The heroes of the Canadian legacy philanthropy story are everyday middle-class people who live in your neighbourhood. While they've been 'donors' throughout their lifetimes, they're seizing this once-in-a-lifetime opportunity to transcend themselves to philanthropist status.

A COHORT PRIMER

As direct marketers, we're no strangers to segmentation. Every fundraiser, and every marketer, knows that the more effectively you can slice and dice an audience, the more effective you'll be. Now, there are all sorts of ways that we can subdivide audiences, but we have found over the years that age is perhaps the most useful, and simplest, way in which we can effectively create audiences to which we can speak more personally and persuasively.

If you're new to the idea of generational cohorts, think of groups of people all born within about 20 years of each other. These groups are moving through time on a big conveyor belt called life. We have five of these groups to consider. Life is coming to the end for the eldest and the size of the group is shrinking. Another one is still being born and growing. And, there are three in the middle that are staying pretty much intact.

These groups are:

1. CIVICS (born before 1946). This is the group that is dwindling in significant numbers.
2. BABY BOOMERS (born 1946 to 1966).
3. GEN X (born 1967 to 1982).
4. MILLENNIALS (born 1982 to 1999).
5. GEN Z (born since 2000). This group is still being born.

Each of these generations came of age in very different times under very different influences. We have different beliefs, values, communications styles, and tastes.

Just think of music for example. A member of the Civic cohort grew up listening to Frank Sinatra and Bing Crosby, while Boomers grew up on the Rolling Stones and Led Zeppelin. Gen Xers came of age with Bruce Springsteen and Madonna. Millennials grew up with the Backstreet Boys and Britney Spears.

SPEAKING TO EACH GENERATION

Here is an introductory tip sheet on how you could try to address the different generations with approaches that are specific to them:

1. **Civics.** This is the last of the loyal, dependable generations. This group by and large respects people in positions of authority and feels a sense of duty and responsibility to support good causes (yep, they can be motivated by guilt!). This is the last cohort that attends religious services with regularity – and its giving motivations are very much based in the Judeo-Christian ethic (love thy neighbor as thyself, for example).

2. **Baby Boomers.** While Civics have very conforming values, Boomers are all about individuality. Boomers place a high importance on identity, and their sense of their own individual brand if you like. While you might talk to a Civic about how '*we as a society need to find a cure for cancer*,' you might say to the Boomer '*your support for the fight against cancer will show the world your commitment to this important cause.*'

3. **Gen Xers.** While Boomers came from Leave It To Beaver families for the most part, Gen X was the first cohort in history where single-parent families were common. While Boomers preached 'free love,' Gen Xers came of age with STIs. The Gen X cohort by and large is more anxious and less trusting than its predecessors.

   There are two major considerations when communicating with a Gen X audience. First, make sure you've got your facts straight. Gen Xers are skeptics, and they want to see your proof. Secondly, your choice of messenger is critical with this group. Gen Xers are most influenced by their peers – so rather than getting your CEO to say how great you are, get a donor in her 40s to do it for you. Barack Obama had huge success using peer-to-peer persuasion with Gen Xers during both his Presidential campaigns.

4. **Millennials.** This cohort (the children of the Baby Boomers) grew up with digital technology and doesn't feel the least bit intimidated by innovation. This is also the generation that has no memory of the Cold War or the nuclear threats that existed between the USA and the USSR.

On the one hand, Millennials feel that older generations have given them a world that is broken. On the other hand, this generation has the confidence to feel that they can fix it once the rest of us get out of the way. There are three key elements to communicating effectively with Millennials:

- The content of your message must be absolutely real and authentic. This cohort can sniff out corporate-speak propaganda a mile away.

- You must be very thoughtful in selecting the right channel to reach the Millennial you're targeting. This cohort grew up in a multichannel world, and they stick with their own media preferences.

- You must tailor your message to fit the channel you're using. You must not cut and paste direct mail copy to create an e-appeal for example. If you want to communicate successfully with Millennials, you must become something akin to multilingual – except your languages might be texting, Snapchat, website, email, and YouTube.

SHOW ME THE MONEY!

Now it's time to narrow our focus to the two cohorts that matter most – the Civics and the Baby Boomers.

When it comes to legacy gifts, only two of our five generations play a significant role (at this time).

According to our most recent generation-specific research which was undertaken in the *2014 State of the Legacy Nation*:

- Civics account for 34% of legacy gifts (even though they only account for 11% of the population!).

- Baby Boomers account for 50% of all legacy gifts (and keep in mind that millions of Canadian Boomers have yet to make their bequests).

- Gen Xers have left 16%, and Millennials have left about 1%.

- (We haven't measured Gen Z yet – so stay tuned for that in five years or so.)

Civics and Boomers combined account for 83% of all legacy gifts. So unless you have an unlimited budget, you'd be wise to stay focused on these cohorts.

MEET KEVIN

Let's look at an example of someone who would fit our legacy profile. This person – who is on the 'border' between the Civic and Boomer cohorts – is actually based on someone we know.

Kevin is a 74-year-old widower who lives in Ottawa. He has four grown children and four grandchildren. He has been retired for 10 years and lives on a modest income of about $35,000 per year. He wears sweatpants most days, cuts his own hair, and does his grocery shopping at Price Chopper (a discount grocery chain in the area). Kevin makes about five donations a year to some charities that he cares about. But, those donations only collectively amount to about $250 or $300 each per year. By most standards, Kevin would appear as a very ordinary donor on a fundraiser's radar screen.

But let's look deeper. Kevin owns a house in a small rural town an hour outside the city and a condominium in the downtown core. He also has some investments. Kevin's net worth is over $1 million.

As Kevin decides to revise his will, he decides to divide his $1 million+ estate into 10 equal shares. Each of his four children and each of his four grandchildren will receive a share. The remaining two shares will go to charities that he cares deeply about:

- The first will go to The Ottawa Hospital Foundation. Kevin's late wife was cared for at The Ottawa Hospital during the last year of her life, and he has always felt intense gratitude for the care she received during her last months.

- The second will go to the Canada Aviation and Space Museum. Kevin enlisted in the Canadian Air Force right out of high school and his friends from his early Air Force days are still his best friends more than 50 years later. Kevin's favourite Sunday pastime is to take his grandkids to the Museum to look at the planes and imagine themselves flying.

Let's stop and look at Kevin through one more lens. During his lifetime, he made about 20 gifts of about $50 to both the hospital and the museum. His lifetime giving to each institution amounted to about $1,000. Yet, when his estate is settled, the hospital and the museum will each receive bequests in excess of $100,000.

DONOR LOYALTY

We can hear what you're thinking:

"It's all well and good to know that people aged 60+ who have paid off their mortgages are my best legacy prospects. But how am I supposed to FIND them?"

Relax. You already have everything you need in your database to find your prospects.

Let's go back to the early days of *Iceberg Philanthropy*, more than a decade ago. Back then, our first step with legacy clients was to do a survey-type exercise where annual donors would self-identify as legacy gift prospects by answering three key questions a certain way:

- They would say that the client charity was one of their three favourite charities of all those they support.

- They would say that they thought that charitable gifts in wills were 'a good idea.'

- They would indicate that they didn't feel compelled to give all of their estate to children or grandchildren – meaning that they were open to making some of their estates' value available to charities.

Now, this method of prospect identification was very effective. But it was also expensive. Often, our clients wanted to invest their money in persuading prospects to give more than they wanted to identify their prospects in the first place.

Then, some sweet serendipity happened.

As we continued to do these prospect identification surveys with our legacy clients, we started finding a high correlation between the three positive indicators above and their giving behaviour.

Here's what we found:

- First and foremost, direct mail donors make the best legacy prospects. If your charity has a direct mail program and you're not actively marketing legacy gifts to those donors, you're leaving a lot of money on the table!

- We found that, pretty much every time, exactly one-quarter of the donor file self-identified as qualified legacy gift prospects. We have enough experience with this to assert to you that you should be actively and regularly marketing legacy giving to about a quarter of your donor database.

- One interesting side-note: We found that donors who had the honorific prefix 'Miss' make really good legacy prospects, regardless of their giving history. If you have someone who uses 'Miss' as her prefix, talk to her about her will!

- The key predictor of legacy giving is donor loyalty over time. So, rather than looking for lots of money, we're looking for the repeated *behaviour* of giving over an extended period of time.

We could write a chapter on data selection here, but we won't. Let's just offer a simulated choice between two donors.

We'll give you the giving profile of each donor and ask you to determine which one would make the better legacy prospect.

- Donor #1 has made gifts of $1,000 in 2008, 2010, 2013, and 2014. Her total giving is $4,000.

- Donor #2 made her first gift to your charity in 1998. Since then, she has made 17 direct mail gifts to you, averaging $35 per gift. Her total giving is $595.

Which donor would you choose? Many people would intuitively choose Donor #1 because of the money, namely $4,000. Experience has taught us, however, that Donor #2 is a better legacy prospect because she has given 17 gifts – as opposed to 4. Donor #2 is the more loyal donor.

Remember, it's the giving *behaviour* that matters here, more so than the total money given!

As an aside, major gift donors generally do not make the best legacy prospects. These folks have cash to donate today and often are looking for an immediate tax benefit. When looking through the expectancy files of our clients, most have only been able to persuade 1-10% of major gift donors into making a gift in their will as well.

There are some other juicy tidbits to consider, if you can access the information. For example:

- People who attend religious services with any regularity are far more likely to make a charitable bequest than people who don't go to church, temple, mosque, or synagogue.

- Canadians whose first language is English are far more likely to make legacy gifts than Canadians whose first language is French.

- People with no children are actually not more likely to make legacy gifts than people with children.

However, people with no children make gifts on average that are twice as large as people with children.

But let's not get lost in the weeds of detail here. There are a few simple ideas to keep in mind as you move forward:

- Most legacy gifts come from people over the age of 60.

- The lion's share of the wealth resides in the value of houses that are paid for by some 6 million Canadians.

- Direct mail donors (if you have them) are fantastic legacy prospects.

- Loyal giving behaviour (and not the amount of money given) is the key clue your database can give you to help you identify legacy gift prospects.

There are literally millions of people much like Kevin in Canada today. In your community. In your neighbourhood. In your database. They're not doing anything to attract attention to themselves, so you have to do a little work to find them. But the work isn't all that hard. Read on…

CHAPTER 3:
RAINDROPS ON THE ROOF:
TIMING YOUR LEGACY MARKETING

Jane Fonda does a wonderful TED talk on the subject of life's third act. Fonda puts forward the case that life, just like a Shakespearean play, takes place within a three-act format.

In the typical three-act format, we meet our characters, get to know the setting, get introduced to the conflict, feel the tension build, experience the crisis, resolve the crisis, and come back home again.

In life, our three acts go something like this, according to Fonda:

- Act One takes place from birth to about age 30. We grow, we learn, we test, and we become. This is the stage during which we develop into the person we're going to be for the rest of our lives.

- Act Two is the stage of our lives that occurs roughly between age 30 and age 60. These are our busy, productive years. This is the phase when we grow professionally, acquire whatever material wealth we will have, possibly raise our children. This middle stage of life is all about achievement and being productive.

- In Act Three, between ages 60 and 90, we've reached our career peak. Our kids are raised and our house is paid for. The pressure to be productive lifts, and we have the opportunity to turn our attention away from constant work and effort. During this last phase in life, we answer our big questions and resolve our life's purpose.

This idea of life stages is not new. There have been societies with similar ideas and traditions for thousands of years. This cycle of birth, growth, productivity, contemplation, and resolution seems to be a universal theme in the human experience.

MAKING THE WILL

Let's go back to Jacqueline and Wilf, who you met in the introduction to this book. You may recall that they made their first wills during the time when they were in the thick of their family formation. They had recently married. They had bought their first house (and took out their first mortgage). Their third child in five years had been born.

You may recognize this stage in life yourself. Suddenly you're not just young, independent, and free. There are others who love you and depend on you. You have become a provider – and your material security doesn't just involve you anymore. You simply have more at stake.

This is the classic time of life when many, if not most, people make their first wills. The three most common triggers for a first will are a marriage or loving partnership, the birth of a child, or the purchase of a first home.

But let's not confuse will-making with charitable bequest-making. These are two very different animals.

When Jacqueline and Wilf made their first wills, they needed everything they owned to go to the surviving spouse or their children. They needed to make sure there was a named guardian for their children should they die at the same time. After all, they didn't have much in the way of wealth yet – and the bank still owned way more of their house than they did!

Some planned giving fundraisers think that an optimal time to approach supporters about legacy gifts is when they are first making their wills. We don't agree. At the end of the first act of life, people for the most part just don't have enough wealth yet to consider giving some of it to charities. Those gifts will come – but not just yet.

MAKING THE CHARITABLE BEQUEST

Now, let's fast-forward Jacqueline and Wilf ahead about 30 years – from the end of their first acts to the end of their second acts. We now have a very different story on a number of fronts:

- Jacqueline and Wilf are now about 60 years of age. They're crossing the bridge to their third act.

- They have managed to pay off their mortgage and the house is theirs free and clear. And not only that – the $22,500 house they bought in 1968 is worth more than $410,000 30 years later. Jacqueline and Wilf have wealth.

- Their kids are grown, educated, and gone. In fact, grandkids are on the way.

- Lastly, Jacqueline has not only had her own breast lump, but has lost a sister to breast cancer. She's committed to a cause. She is on a philanthropic mission.

It is these factors that affect legacy gift-giving. Entering the third act. Finishing the job of raising children. Achieving total home ownership. And caring deeply about a cause. These are the factors that trigger people to leave gifts to charities in their wills.

THE GOLDEN TIME – AS THE THIRD ACT UNFOLDS

Today, Jacqueline is about halfway through her life's third act. She's in her 70s and hopefully has 15 or 20 years left to enjoy her grandkids, and maybe even great-grandkids.

Jacqueline updated her will a year after Wilf's death. She added two new grandchildren as beneficiaries and included her hospital in Brandon that had taken such wonderful care of Wilf in his final months.

Soon, Jacqueline will amend her will once more. She has another grandchild. She has lost a brother to whom she had left a small bequest. And, she wants to increase her bequest to the Canadian Cancer Society because her commitment to the cause has grown.

THE LEGACY GIVING SWEET SPOT

Many people begin updating their wills with some regularity after their 60th birthday, or as retirement approaches and takes place. This is the time in their lives when you need to be talking to those who have been loyal to your cause about bequests to your organization.

Most charitable bequest-makers don't make appointments with their lawyers just so that they can make a gift to your charity. Rather, they've built a list over the past five years or so and you need to be on that list. In most cases, we believe that changes in family circumstances – like the birth of grandchildren and the death of spouses or siblings – are the primary triggers.

Here's the kicker:

Your legacy prospect will add you to her will on her schedule – not yours! She might update her will next week, next month, next year, or four years from now. You do NOT get to speed up that process. But, you DO need to be present in her mind when she makes that call to book an appointment with her lawyer.

WHAT WE DO WRONG

Fundraisers often think of legacy gift marketing in terms of short-term campaigns. They secure some funding in their budget for the current fiscal year. Someone (often a consultant claiming planned giving expertise) tells them that they should send out one mailing and follow that mailing up with a phone call, or develop an email campaign with 4 touchpoints. It's quick. It's easy. It's not *too* expensive. And, best of all, you get some fast results that you can report to your Executive Director or Board.

There are two fundamental flaws with this kind of thinking.

First off, these types of campaigns will absolutely help you uncover existing expectancies. You'll be very successful in getting folks who have already left you a gift in their will to let you know. But your legacy marketing efforts in this particular campaign will have had nothing to do with them leaving a gift in their will. So really, you haven't accomplished anything but finding out about money that's already coming in. And even worse, you've had very little to do with getting prospects who haven't given yet to think on, or even make a gift in their will.

Secondly, this singular two or three-month 'campaign' approach is built to suit the consultant and the charity staff – but *not* the loyal donor who's a legacy gift prospect.

These results are great for the bottom line and validating investment into planned giving. One new expectancy can justify the entire investment in this particular planned giving campaign. But you're not building a pipeline.

To be truly donor-centric means to build programs around the donor and her reality – and your donors' reality is that they update their wills about every five years. And, to stretch it even further, your donor might include you in her will two updates from now. That's TEN years in the future instead of five!

So, if you bang out a six-week campaign now, the odds are that your donor will have completely forgotten about any of its content by the time she goes to see her lawyer in two or three years. Money wasted. Time wasted. Opportunity missed.

There's a better way to do this.

RAINDROPS ON THE ROOF

So, let's toss the campaign aside and build a program instead. A program that's designed around your donors. A program that's going to last. A program that's going to work!

The image that sums up our strategy is that of raindrops on a roof. We live in Ottawa, Ontario and we get two kinds of rain in the summertime...

Often in the late afternoon, a thunderstorm will roll in from the west. The sky will get black and the wind will pick up. And suddenly, a torrent of rain comes crashing down in all its fury, accompanied by a symphony of thunder and lightning.

Then, as soon as it began, the storm is over. Fifteen minutes later, the sky returns to blue and all is right with the world again.

But we also have a different kind of rain. The kind of soft, gentle rain that falls all day, and maybe all night too. Surely, you've spent a summer vacation day indoors – maybe at your cottage – on a day like that. You're playing board games inside and listening to the soft and steady drumbeat of raindrops on the roof.

That's the sound that we want to have stick in your brain from this day forward. Whenever you think of your planned giving program, we want you to think of that rainy day at the cottage. We want your donors to hear those raindrops – and we want consistent legacy persuasion messages to *be* those raindrops.

Smart legacy marketers pick the best available audience of prospects (recall that these are likely your most longtime, loyal supporters) and send them consistent, repeated legacy persuasion and cultivation messages over a long period of time. And, by 'long' we mean five to ten years.

Now, your instinct might be to say to yourself *'That's way too long. My donors will get sick of hearing this stuff over and over from me!'* We get it. We feel that way too sometimes. But that instinct is just plain wrong.

If you'd like an estimate, we'd say that you'd want to put between four and six messages per year in front of your prospect audience over a period of about seven years. That's assuming that a prospect will hear about 35 legacy messages from you before she actually goes and makes her gift.

HERE'S THE KICKER

We've been in the legacy business for more than 20 years now – and we've learned a thing or two along the way. One of the biggest lessons we've learned is that, at most charities, legacy giving is important – but not urgent.

The raindrop strategy we're asking you to embark on involves small first steps. You don't need a big change of heart from your Executive Director or a big policy shift from your Board. What you do need is your own resolve to take those first small steps. Make those first raindrops fall. And then have the discipline, the patience, and the resolve to stay at it until the money starts rolling in.

When people start to notice the money in a few years, you're away to the races.

CHAPTER 4:
CRAFTING YOUR LEGACY STRATEGY AND GUIDING PRINCIPLES

Now it's time to turn our attention to what you should actually be doing to plan and execute an effective, efficient – and highly profitable – legacy gift marketing program.

But, it's not time to share recipes just yet. Before we start getting into the 'how to' instructional stuff, it's important that we take some time to really think through the overall direction of your program. We want you to set ambitious goals and come up with a strategy that allows you to achieve those goals. Once we have the right strategy in place, you'll be ready to choose the mixture of activities and audiences that will propel you forward.

So friends, this chapter is about strategy.

In our experience, organizations that launch campaigns and programs without clearly thinking through their strategies are very likely to squander a lot of time, energy, and money along the way. None of us wants to do that – so let's take the time to set a proper strategy first. Then, and only then, we'll plan to invest money and time where it will do the most good.

WHAT GREAT STRATEGISTS AND LEADERS DO (AND YOU SHOULD DO TOO!)

Truly strategic leadership entails doing five steps in sequence:

1. Learn everything possible about your environment, your audience, and your competition. Get to know the lay of the land. Leave no stone unturned. (Spoiler alert: reading this book is a part of this stage!)

2. Decide on your strategy and define your win.

3. Make your tactical plan. Now is when you get into the operational and executional details of when, how, where, and by whom your campaign or program will unfold.

4. Execute the plan. Pay attention to detail. Be consistent. Be disciplined.

5. Evaluate outcomes and adjust your plan as new information comes to light.

These five steps are simple. And, they've proven to be effective for more than 2,000 years. Julius Caesar and Alexander the Great followed these steps to win wars. Henry Ford and Steve Jobs used these steps to build businesses. Presidents and Prime Ministers have used these steps to get elected and re-elected. And great fundraisers have followed these steps to raise gazillions of dollars over the years.

Here's the thing. Being a truly strategic leader and/or fundraiser is a pretty simple proposition. But, simple and easy are not the same thing! Sometimes the simplest things can be the most difficult. However, in our experience, being truly strategic always pays rich dividends in the long run.

A STRATEGY IS A SENTENCE

Here's a radical idea for you:

If you truly have a strategy, you can say it in a sentence. And, your sentence will contain four essential components (whose acronym is STAR).

1. SUBJECT: The subject is the one who will benefit from the strategy should it succeed. In terms of legacy giving, the subject is you, your charity, and your fundraising program.

2. TARGET: A strategy is always aimed at someone. Sometimes, that someone is the enemy (military), opposition (politics), competition (business), or audience (marketing).

3. ACTION: This is the singular *idea* that will create the win.

4. RESULT: The outcome of the strategy is your definition of the win.

HOW STEVE JOBS HELPED BUILD AN ICEBERG

Let us give you an example.

In the early days of personal computing, IBM ruled the roost. Almost every personal computer on the planet ran on an IBM-created operating system called MS-DOS. One glance at a computer screen that was running MS-

DOS made it obvious that it was designed by a programmer. You needed to already have a lot of specialized, niche knowledge to use it effectively – and nothing about it was intuitive.

Then, along came two young guys in California named Steve Wozniak and Steve Jobs. They had the radical ideas that personal computers, and their operating systems, could be designed around the *user* and not the *programmer*. Instead of a black screen with blinking numbers, letters, and punctuation marks, the two Steves created a screen that mimicked a desk with file folders on it. Documents could be dragged and deposited (courtesy of a mouse!) into those folders. And, folders could have simple English names like 'budget' or 'projects' (rather than names like C://adm.co.bdg.2018).

Jobs and Wozniak began Apple Computers out of Jobs' parents' garage, and you know the rest. The world's most successful company was built around the idea of making things easy for the user. Apple built a loyal core of customers, and eventually Microsoft (the MS in MS-DOS) had to invent Windows to protect their market share.

If we were to write the strategic sentence for Steve Jobs way back when, it might have looked like this:

Apple will become the world's biggest company by offering user-friendly, attractive, and effective technology products to individual users around the world.

So, let's break this sentence down:

1. The subject is Apple.

2. The target is personal technology users around the world – or people who could become technology users, if the right tool was available to them.

3. The action is offering user-friendly products that people want and can use.

4. The result is becoming the world's most valuable company.

Easy, isn't it?

When you stop and think about it, the planned giving strategy we're proposing in this book is nothing more than taking a page out of the Apple playbook.

THE ICEBERG PHILANTHROPY STRATEGY

When we surveyed the planned giving landscape back in 2003, we found two important things:

1. There are millions of middle-class people (primarily everyday homeowners) who were making bequests, thinking of making bequests, or open to the idea of making bequests.

2. Fundraisers were talking about planned giving to donors as if those donors were sophisticated millionaire philanthropists. There was lots of focus on planning, finances, and tax avoidance as opposed to the charity's cause and mission.

When we wrote *Iceberg Philanthropy,* we wanted to communicate bequest giving to the 90% of legacy donors who were not sophisticated philanthropists. We posited a simple, emotive, and story-based planned giving strategy. We talk about wills only (where about 90-95% of all planned giving revenue comes from) and none of the other planned giving vehicles like life insurance, annuities, or charitable remainder trusts. And, we stay focused on the *why* of the gift rather than the *how* (we'll talk more about the 40-30-20-10 Golden Rule in Chapter 6: Storytelling for a Legacy Audience).

Let's review the strategy that our book *Iceberg Philanthropy* so successfully introduced to the philanthropic world in 2007.

We'll look at each of the four elements before we construct our sentence:

1. The subject is you and your organization.
2. The target is your pool of loyal donors, volunteers, members, and supporters.
3. The action is a marketing approach that is truly donor-centric. It will make it as easy, meaningful, and joyful as possible for a supporter to decide to leave you a bequest.
4. The result is some degree of revenue growth over a certain period of time.

So here's what the legacy strategy sentence could look like for a fictional charity like Awesome Birding Canada (or your organization if you want to substitute your own name).

> *'Awesome Birding Canada will add 20% to our annual net revenues by offering our donors and supporters a consistent, gift-in-will-focused, story-based legacy gift marketing program over the next ten years.'*

So, what might your strategic sentence look like? We welcome you to cut and paste as much as you like from Apple and *Iceberg Philanthropy*.

WHY GUIDING PRINCIPLES ARE SUCH A GREAT IDEA

But, as you likely know, it goes so much deeper than just a sentence. Once you've laid out your strategy, you need to get folks on board – and if you don't do it early, you can find yourself in a world of hurt down the road.

After more than 15 years of working with charities in the area of legacy giving, we have, in recent years, come up with a great tool that can help you do this.

The end result is a simple one-page (maximum) document. It consists of a strategic sentence (which follows the STAR approach to strategy) followed by about six to ten key principles that are listed as bullet points of one or two sentences each.

Think of your statement of guiding principles as your legacy program's manifesto. It sets out the rules and parameters within which you will wage your program. These principles are as important in what they say you will *not* do as much as what you *will* do.

For example, let's say you select as a guiding principle that your program will market gifts in wills only, because 95% of legacy money comes from wills. You're not just saying that you're going to focus on wills – you're also saying that you're not going to use up your precious program resources talking about gifts of insurance, charitable gift annuities, or charitable remainder trusts.

The principles you select will draw your map to success. And, by implication, your map will tell you all the places you intend *not* to go. This will become very useful down the road – especially when distractions start popping up!

It's important that we stress to you that in creating your statement of guiding principles, the process is often more important than the product. If you do this work properly, you will draw everybody who counts into this conversation. You'll engage Board members, executive leadership, senior finance people, and other fundraisers.

The key is that everyone be exposed to these ideas early on – and that they agree to your strategy before you start executing your tactics. Spending some time and effort on this work is smart leadership on your part. Trust us, you'll spend a penny now to save a pound later!

At the end of the process, you'll have a one-page document, as well as consensus on the content of that document. We encourage you to ensure that everyone has a copy and that you refer to it whenever you're reporting at staff meetings or providing board updates.

What you're really doing with your guiding principles process and product is creating a culture around your legacy gift marketing program. You're laying a solid foundation that will last for decades to come. Professionally speaking, you'll also be creating a legacy for yourself that you'll be able to take great pride in for many years!

SO, WHAT DO THESE PRINCIPLES LOOK LIKE?

Every organization is unique and each is in its own place in the evolution of its legacy gift marketing program. Having said that, if you're following our approach, there are probably some principles that you're already aware of, like the following:

- Stay focused on the will.

- Persuade the donor *why* they should make a bequest, rather than instructing them on *how* to do it.

- Use storytelling to create an emotional, autobiographical impulse to give.

Some of these guiding principles, like the ones above, are self-evident and clear. Others though, may be a little less obvious:

- You may want to decide if your primary emphasis is on getting existing bequesters to raise their hands and reveal their gifts to you or persuading loyal donors to actually make bequests. (Our preference is almost always the latter.)

- You may want to articulate a principle that defines the role of the legacy fundraiser vis-à-vis the allied professionals who provide financial counsel to your donors. We often see planned giving fundraisers who wander across the line between charity ambassadorship and donor financial advisor.

- If you have a marketing and communications department that will be designing your legacy materials (print and/or digital), you might want to state up front that your audience is aged about 70 years old – and designs must be simple and bold, use large font, and feature dark type against white backgrounds.

The guiding principles we develop are unique to each charity we work with, their planned giving strategy, and their environment. The above section should give you a good idea on some of the things to consider when drafting your very own principles.

Once you have these principles all drafted, and you have buy-in from everyone who helped to create them, be sure to share a final copy.

MULTIPLE PRIORITIES

It's important that you and your team get very clear about what you're trying to accomplish with your legacy gift marketing program before you take your first steps.

To some people, identifying those donors who have already made a bequest is the name of the game. To others, legacy marketing should be an exercise in prospect identification and qualification. And to others, legacy communications is all about persuasion, without worrying a lot about counting heads. After all, up to 90% of bequest donors won't tell us — so maybe these fundraisers have a point.

Which leads us to the question of measurement and metrics. As you set up your program, how will you determine if you're successful? There are at least three ways to measure your program's performance, and the emphasis on each will change as your legacy work grows and matures:

- In the early stages, you might want to put your greatest emphasis on prospect identification. In other words, you're trying to get people to put their hands up and say, "*Yes, I'm interested in the idea of making a bequest.*"

- Two or three years into your program, your emphasis will probably shift from identifying prospects to confirming expectancies. This means that you're looking for people to confirm to you in some way that they have included your charity in their wills.

- And, of course, we find ourselves counting the money! Some five to seven years into your legacy program, you should start relying primarily on actual legacy dollars in the door as your key success metric.

Now, we're not encouraging you to get overly bureaucratic about this stuff, but it's good to have these conversations before you begin doing the work. It's amazing how we can all start from different assumptions and arrive at different conclusions unless we have an explicit conversation at the get-go.

Once you've gone through this process, your strategy is set. Your leadership, colleagues, and stakeholders are in line with your plan. Now, it's finally time to dig into the science of legacy giving and begin to explore your future tactical options.

CHAPTER 5:
THE GIVING BRAIN

Hopefully, Jacqueline's journey helped you understand where legacy gifts 'fit' in your donor's life journey. In this chapter, we want to help you get inside your donors' minds, so you can talk about legacy gifts with them a lot more effectively.

THE SUCCESSFUL MARKETER'S FIRST RULE

In the classic marketing book, *Positioning: The Battle for the Mind*, authors Jack Ries and Al Trout talk a lot about the necessity of learning to speak from the outside-in, rather than the inside-out. This is what they mean.

The supplier of a good or service is on the inside of the equation. They know how the product is made and how it works. They know the details of the manufacturing process and the fine points of quality control. They know their competition, their price point, their market share — they know a lot! If they were to start talking about their product, they could probably bore you to tears in no time with a bunch of details you really don't care about.

To talk about a product or service from the outside-in, that same supplier must 'unlearn' almost everything we've just talked about. They must then try to crawl inside the brain of their prospective customer and see the world through her eyes. Almost always, the customer cares about outcomes rather than processes. She wants simple information that's relevant to her.

So, let's imagine that you have a splitting headache and you come across two side-by-side pharmacy counters. The pharmacist at the first counter starts telling you about all of his different pain killing medications, both pharmaceutical and natural. He starts teaching you the difference between ASA and acetaminophen. He starts discussing dosage options – and on and on…

The second pharmacist looks into your pained face and says, *"Take two of these and your headache will be gone in ten minutes."* Now, if you were suffering from a splitting migraine, which pharmacist would you want? It's kind of a no-brainer, isn't it?

As a fundraiser, think of yourself as one of those pharmacists. And, think of your legacy gift prospect as the customer. Which do you think is a smarter strategy? Showing off everything you know about planned giving? Or, telling them about the things that are likely to persuade them to make a bequest to your organization? You'd think the answer would be obvious – and yet a lot of planned giving fundraisers don't get it yet.

Let's start with the science behind legacy giving and take a closer look at the human brain.

THE EVOLUTION OF THE THREE DONOR BRAINS

Close your eyes for a moment and visualize those wooden Russian nesting dolls – some people call them Matryoshka Dolls. Now, visualize your brain as actually being three brains, nesting in turn inside each other.

This is what your brain really is and how it really works. Your brain is actually three separate brains that are interconnected, a model that was developed by neuroscientist Paul MacLean in the 1960s which he called the triune brain. Each of them performs important roles – and it's the combination of these three brains that helped us evolve to where we are today.

The Reptile Brain

When you've looked *way* back into your family tree, have you ever come across the lobe-finned fish? (We didn't think so.)

About 370 million years ago, some fish developed lungs that allowed them to crawl up on land and breathe air. We are descended from these creatures and, in a way, they still live inside us. While our lobe-finned ancestors didn't have big brains compared to ours, their brains were very well-designed for what they had to do.

You see, the lobe-finned fish had a one-track mind; survival was the only goal. Our amphibious ancestors were only concerned with their own survival as individuals, and creating baby lobe-finned fish to sustain the species. This is where our survival instinct lives. Eat. Mate. Fight. Flight.

Now, here's the kicker. You still have this ancient, instinctive brain in your head. It's one of three brains actually. Today, neuromarketers like to call this smallest, but most powerful brain, our reptile brain.

The Mammal Brain

Let's come ahead in time by about 200 million years. Now you have an ancestor who's a mammal. This ancestor gives birth to live young, has fur and an internal skeleton, and nurses its babies. You probably don't know this, but your oldest mammalian ancestor is a little mouse-like creature called the Skinny Shrew, and it lived about 170 million years ago.

One element of the mammal's more advanced evolution (compared to the lobe-finned fish) was the development of a second brain that was located just above the reptile brain. This brain is scientifically referred to as the limbic system, but many neuromarketers refer to it as the mammal brain.

While the reptile brain is focused only on instinct and survival, the mammal brain is somewhat more complex. It's the feeling part of our selves that controls our emotional response. As we evolved from amphibians to apes, our brains were wired with emotional software that we still have and use every day.

We'll come back and talk about emotions in more detail shortly, but the key thing to keep in mind now is this: Our emotional response wiring was programmed into our brains to help us survive.

It's also worth noting that our emotional responses are instant and automatic. They don't involve thinking or decision-making.

The Big Brain

Now, fast forward way ahead to only 1.8 million years ago. It was at this point in your family's history that Homo erectus made her first appearance in world history.

One of the changes that happened between apes and humans was the development of the great big human brain that we have today. This brain is the large pink-grey wrinkly brain that we know from photos and videos.

This part of the human brain – properly known as the neocortex – is far bigger than either the reptile brain or the mammal brain that lives within it. The easiest way to visualize the big brain is that it is our human computer.

It's the neocortex that allows for complex thought in place of instinctive responses. The neocortex lets us use language, which means we can communicate with and learn from each other. The big brain lets us do math, solve puzzles, plan for the future, set priorities, schedule our time, and hundreds of other things that keep us organized, safe, and successful.

The big brain is the brain we usually try to communicate with as fundraisers. We show it graphs and charts. We show philanthropic return on investment. We suggest gift amounts and compare your charity favourably to others that the donor might be considering.

All this is well and good, but…

The fact of life is that the other two brains (reptile and mammal) are more powerful than the big brain, because they're wired for survival. They don't just think about keeping us alive – they actually do it. They function on instinct and immediacy, not careful logic. And if either of them are activated, the big brain won't be the decision-maker.

The Hierarchy

If you want to understand donors in general, and legacy donors in particular, you need to remember this simple hierarchy:

Emotions are more powerful than thoughts. The heart rules the head.

Our instincts are more powerful than either our emotions or our thoughts.

So, the reptile brain rules the roost. Because it's rooted in fight-or-flight, the thing it fears most is death. The mammal brain runs second. It is the emotional engine that helps us to decide what is good and what is bad in the environment around us. Only when our instinctive and emotional brains are at rest does our thinking brain govern what we decide and how we behave.

By the way, this three-level hierarchy doesn't *just* work with donors. It works with spouses, kids, friends, bosses, and co-workers too!

PRIMARY EMOTIONS (WHERE THE MAMMALIAN BRAIN MEETS THE BIG BRAIN)

No doubt, you learned about the primary colours in an elementary school art class when you were a kid. The primary colours (red, yellow, and blue in case you've forgotten) are the base colours from which all others are derived. You know... blue and yellow make green, yellow and red make orange, and so on.

We'll bet that when you were in school, no one taught you about the *primary emotions*. It's worth taking a few moments now to explore these emotions – the language of the mammal brain – because they will come to play a pretty large role in your legacy gift persuasion efforts.

Perhaps the simplest way we can define an emotion is to call it a powerful, immediate response to an event that either threatens or furthers our odds of survival. There are eight primary emotions, which are grouped into four pairs of polar opposites, according to psychologist Robert Plutchik in his wheel of emotions:

- **Fear** is the instinctual urge to run away from something that is dangerous to our survival, while **anger** is the urge to fight something that is trying to take something important to our survival from us.

- **Sadness** is the unpleasant feeling we have when we lose something, whereas **joy** is the positive feeling that reminds us of what is important in our life and experiences we want to have again.

- **Trust** is what connects us to others and underpins the confidence that they will do as expected, whereas **disgust** is the revulsion or profound disapproval of others who act unpredictably or to the detriment of the group, which is rooted in an instinctual avoidance of contagion or disease.

- **Surprise** is how we're startled in new situations or due to an unexpected event, whereas **anticipation** is the pleasure, anxiety, or excitement we feel when we look forward to a planned event.

When you stop and think about it, you'll realize just how much your emotions still govern your decisions and behaviours. How about losing your temper at some jerk in rush hour traffic? Eating a pint of ice cream because you feel sad on the anniversary of a parent's death? Making sure all your belongings are together because being invited in for a one-on-one meeting with your boss sparked fear that you would be fired? Telling your children you'd make whatever they want for dinner because you were elated after reading the great report cards they just brought home?

Our day-to-day behaviours are still very much governed by our emotions. It's like making the choice to avoid shopping at a particular grocery store because it's too far away, the produce is of poor quality, the prices are too high, and because there was that one time your car got hit in the parking lot by a teenager who let a grocery cart get away.

Is your car likely to get hit again by a rogue grocery cart next time you head to the store? No. But it made you so mad that it happened that you see red every time you think about going back there. This is the mammalian brain response. It's the emotional trigger that's driving your behaviour.

But when you try to make sense of your behaviour (to either yourself or others), the neocortex has already taken over. You've given yourself the rationale that this particular grocery store is too far away. Reality check: All three stores are within 5km of your house. You argue that the quality of the produce at this store is substandard. Reality check: It's not fantastic, but it's no worse than what you'd find at the other two stores and they all need to up their game. You are certain that the prices too high. As it turns out, this point is true. This store is more expensive... but mostly on pre-packaged food and you're trying to eat less of it anyway.

The real reason you won't shop ever again at this particular store is because you're angry with what happened. Your mammalian brain fears that this will happen again. But your modern big brain can't function with only emotional decision making. It needs rationale. So you come up with a list of reasons to explain your behaviour. Your big brain is playing catch-up to your mammal brain, because you need logic to make sense of the world.

We give to charities, non-profits, and causes from emotional responses too. The impulse to give a gift today is driven by that emotional mammalian brain. You might feel sad for the abused puppy at the local humane society. Or you could feel anger at a story told by a woman in a shelter for survivors of domestic violence. You could feel happy reading a charity newsletter that tells you how your donation was used, and decide to give again. You might feel fear at the prospect of a possible cancer diagnosis in your future and give to your hospital so that it can invest in engineering immune cells and vaccine research to end leukemia.

Good fundraisers know how to pull the emotional trigger and speak to the mammalian brain rather than the big brain to get that annual gift. Then, the big brain will take over and help the donor make sense of why they chose to give. But really, the choice has already been made.

The abused puppy at the shelter? You give because you love animals, always had dogs growing up, and would never want to have an animal put down when rehabilitation is an option. The survivor of domestic violence? You remember hearing about the École Polytechnique massacre on the news when you were 10, that you helped a friend escape a controlling boyfriend in your early 20s, and are raising your daughter today to be strong and hope that she never gets caught in the cycle of domestic violence. Fear of a cancer diagnosis? You watched several people in your partner's family die of blood cancers, then your partner dies of leukemia, and heaven forbid you or one of your children get diagnosed with it too.

Now, let's extend our thinking about our primary emotions and how they developed to help us survive. Not only are we human beings emotional creatures, we are also the most social creatures on the planet. In fact, many researchers believe that human beings are at the top of the food chain because of our ability to form communities together and specialize as individuals within those communities.

Of course, we're not at the top of the food chain for our physical attributes. There are lots of other mammals that are faster, bigger, and stronger. And, while we humans possess the greatest intellectual capacity of all the species, it's arguably our ability to live in sophisticated groups that is our greatest evolutionary advantage.

Now, let's link our social hardwiring to our primary emotions. Over millions of years, we evolved and developed the ability to instinctively think, feel, and act not only to survive as individuals – but also, to survive as communities. This means that we don't only feel fear when we're threatened, but we also can feel fear when someone in our social group is threatened. This is the evolutionary root of empathy.

The dictionary defines empathy as *the ability to understand and share the feelings of another*. And, when you get right down to it, empathy is the evolutionary root of philanthropy. We love humankind (our fellow human group members). We share their joys, fears, and sorrows. We do what we can for each other to alleviate pain and to elevate happiness and joy.

In the vast majority of cases, empathy is at the core of why your donors choose to give you money, and why your volunteers choose to give you time.

If your brain retains only one piece of information from this chapter, we hope it's this: The heart creates the *impulse* to give before the brain can make the *decision* to give.

MEET RUSSELL JAMES

If we know that the emotional impulse of the mammalian brain is what truly drives a donor to make a gift (a gift that the rational big brain makes sense of after the fact), what does this mean when it comes to legacy giving?

If you aren't already familiar with his work, we'd like to introduce you to Dr. Russell James. He is a very original and innovative man indeed. After obtaining a B.A. in Economics and a Law Degree, he received his Ph.D. in Consumer Economics at the University of Missouri. He then pursued an academic career which finds him today serving as the Director of Graduate Studies in Charitable Financial Planning at Texas Tech University.

We first came across Russell James at a Canadian Association of Gift Planners Conference, and we were blown away by what he was doing. This guy was actually hooking up MRI machines to donors' brains while they were thinking and talking about making legacy gifts! He began documenting the empirical neuroscience of legacy philanthropy – and his findings teach us some powerful lessons.

We'll refer to Russell James again before we're done, but for now let's focus in on one of his key insights into the psychology of bequest giving and how it's entirely different from what sparks a donor to make a regular one-time annual donation.

THE AUTOBIOGRAPHICAL BRAIN

In almost all areas of philanthropy and charitable giving, neuroscience has identified the part of the brain that triggers the gift. As we've already discussed, in most types of giving, it's the *empathy centre* – that feeling part of the brain – that is fired up when a gift is being contemplated.

When we're in empathetic mode, we're understanding and sharing the feelings of others. Their emotions become our emotions, and our mammal brain is triggered. It makes total sense that someone who is feeling someone else's pain or fear or loneliness would be willing to give to ease the suffering. For the most part, empathy is key to philanthropy.

But, Russell James has shown that the charitable bequest doesn't come from the empathy centre of the brain. It comes from the brain's *autobiographical centre*. Put another way, the empathy centre of the brain is probably why your donors give to you – but it's the autobiographical centre that's going to elevate that support to the decision to make a legacy gift.

To get a bit technical for a moment, James's fMRI research shows that when a donor receives bequest messages, the lingual gyrus and the precuneus areas of the brain are activated. The lingual gyrus is part of the visual system, which is associated with internal visualization. Damage to this area of the brain can cause you to lose your ability to dream. The precuneus, otherwise known as the mind's eye, is activated when we take a look at ourselves from the position of an outside observer. That is, taking a third-person perspective.

Think about this in writing. You could say, "*Today I cleaned out my kitchen cupboards while listening to an old album from The Tragically Hip (obviously, it was Fully Completely)*." Or, if you were to take the third-person perspective, you would say, "*Today, [INSERT YOUR NAME] cleaned out [INSERT YOUR NAME]'s kitchen cupboards*."

When you combine the functioning of these two areas of the brain — the visualizing and the self-reflecting — it's what you'd call *visualized autobiographical processing*.

Now, add to this another piece of James's research, where he asked people to look at photos from across their lifespan. When participants were shown images that were vividly memorable — think something like a photo of them with their parents and siblings dressed in their fanciest Easter clothing in front of the childhood home — the lingual gyrus and precuneus parts of the brain were activated. But, so was the hippocampus.

Now, the hippocampus is part of the brain that's related to memory recall. It's also *not* part of the brain that was activated in James's earlier experiments.

This is important science for us in understanding the autobiographical brain and bequest giving. In a donor's brain, vivid autobiographical experiences BUT NOT memory recall is activated when thinking about legacy giving. That is because during the bequest decision-making process, you are mentally completing the final chapter of your visualized autobiography in the future. In your mind's eye, you are writing the part of the story you haven't lived yet. You're not remembering the past, or events you have lived, when in this autobiographical state.

Instead, this is the place in the brain where you are constructing the story of your life. You are holding up a mirror and looking at yourself (that's the third-person perspective again). It's where you weave together the events of your life and your personal characteristics to form a cohesive whole. Our autobiographical brain wants to answer the questions *'Has my life been worthwhile?'* and *'When it's all said and done, will my life's journey have been worth it?'*. It also asks *'How will I be remembered after I'm gone?.'*

So, it's pretty simple when you get right down to it. The autobiographical brain asks the existential questions. And, the charitable bequest is one of the answers to those questions. The legacy gift affirms the character and goodness of the donor – and casts a vote in favour of judging a life to have been well-lived.

Note on the above: James would caution us that this research is the first foray into understanding charitable bequest decision making from a charitable perspective, and these are hypotheses to help understand the brain mechanism captured on the fMRI. This is further supported by previous research which speaks to the plausibility of his work, but by no means does he want us to think it's a settled issue.

WHEN THE MORTALITY ELEPHANT TROMPS INTO THE ROOM

There is a huge psychological (and often, spiritual) threshold most people have to cross before they're ready to make a gift in their wills: *They need to truly accept their own mortality. They need to truly and fundamentally accept the reality that they will die.*

Now, you might be thinking that this is a very odd thing for us to say! Of course, we all know from the time we're young children that people die.

But for some reason that we don't yet understand, while we know that everyone will die, at the same time we believe in our subconscious brain that we're immortal. We can't actually imagine dying. We can't actually picture a world without us in it. We can't imagine saying goodbye forever – and we can't imagine checking out of the hotel called life.

Dr. Russell James calls this the first stage defence of death avoidance, and there are the five Ds we all employ to avoid thinking about our inevitable deaths: distract, differentiate, deny, delay, and depart.

- Distract: I'm too busy to think about that right now.
- Differentiate: It doesn't apply to me (I'm in good health, I exercise, I eat well).
- Deny: The risk of this happening now is overstated.
- Delay: I will absolutely think about it…later.
- Depart: I am not going to think about this at all.

But then, something happens. Sometime in our life's journey, the truth of our own mortality begins to leak into our conscious and subconscious awareness. We begin to truly accept that the time we have left is limited. We begin to deeply accept the hard reality of our own finality.

Do you remember Jane Fonda's metaphor of life in three acts? Well, our acceptance of our own mortality seems to universally happen as we cross the threshold into our third and final act of life.

There are several life events that could trigger or reinforce this deep shift in our outlook on life. A 60th birthday. Retirement. The birth of a first grandchild. Finding a lump on your breast or an odd-shaped mole on your shoulder. Watching your spouse get sick. Losing a parent, a sibling, or a friend who was your age.

When we wrote *Iceberg Philanthropy* back in 2007, we did some research into mortality and people's acceptance of it. We found an article in the Canadian Journal of Palliative Medicine that made an interesting case. The authors contended that we truly accept our own mortality as we begin to experience the deaths of others in our age cohort. So, once you've been to the memorial service – or read the obituary – for someone from your high school class, someone you had kids in daycare with, or a cousin who was your age, it hits you that this will be your fate someday.

To be practical, we have chosen age 60 as the age when we assume that people in the middle of the bell curve reach this stage in their lives. Now, any bell curve has outliers. If you lost your spouse at 46, you're likely further along in your mortality acceptance process that others in your age cohort. Conversely, if you're still unscathed by the deaths of others at age 65, maybe your own process hasn't started yet. Having said that, choosing age 60 as a qualifier has served our clients well over the years.

SECOND-STAGE DEATH DEFENCE

While the first stage of "death avoidance" keeps your donor from crafting their will in the first place, it's the second stage of "symbolic immortality" that's key for whether or not charity is included in the very estate plans they go on to make. Dr. Russell James's research would tell us that this is exceptionally critical for getting your legacy messaging just right, and we'd agree.

Symbolic immortality is the concept that some part of one's self will continue to exist after death — whether that be your name, your family, your community, your achievements, your values, or your life goals. Where in the first stage, you avoid death by not thinking about it, in the second stage, you avoid death by finding ways to metaphorically live forever.

There is a way of thinking about death that comes from ancient traditions in Mexico, where Día de los Muertos, or day of the dead, is still celebrated today. The idea is that we actually experience three deaths:

- The first death occurs when we draw our last breath.
- The second death occurs when our body is lowered into the ground.
- The third and final death occurs when there is no one left alive to remember us.

You can see that an act of legacy philanthropy could be interpreted as a means of extending one's third life, and ensuring that one's name will continue to be spoken – and that our life will be remembered.

When you've admitted to yourself that you will die, your brain then moves on to this stage of death defence which is focussed on the parts of ourselves that are not mortal. This stage is all about the future autobiographical self: what will remain of our lives after death. This might be tangible (something you create that outlives you) or intangible (like a loved one's memories of you).

Based on research from Dr. Ernest and Isadora Rosenbaum, who were pioneers in cancer support at Stanford Medical, there are four types of symbolic immortality. The first three are most universal in the human experience:

1. Biologic symbolic immortality: Our life continues through our children, grandchildren, and family. This is about more than passing on one's genes – it's about being remembered for who we were and what we stood for. This is a legacy of values, traditions, and an approach to life passed from one generation to the next.

2. Theological or religious symbolic immortality: Many, but not all, religions and spiritual practices hold a belief in life after death. The afterlife, with an immortal soul, is an ancient mythological theme, involving death, rebirth, and resurrection.

3. Creative symbolic immortality: Your work on this planet and your contributions to society can outlive you. This might be something concrete and measurable: a work of art, a scientific discovery, a piece of revolutionary policy. You can also create an impact in someone else's life through benevolent acts, for which they will remember you. Through creative symbolic immortality, we live on through

.

accomplishments which will be remembered for generations to come.

4. Symbolic immortality of nature: If you've ever seen an episode of The Walking Dead, you'll notice that everywhere you look, nature is reclaiming the world. Buildings crumble, fences fall, and bridges collapse at the hands of nature's persistence. By its very nature (no pun intended), our environment will exist long, long after we have come and gone.

Symbolic immortality is the highest, or most extreme form, of autobiographical heroism, according to James. It's the concept that we like to see ourselves as having positive and meaningful lives and that this is reflected by our life stories. For fundraisers, it's how we can speak to biological, theological, or creative symbolic immortality that matters most in crafting our messaging.

It's important to note that symbolic immortality requires a social foundation. It's not something we can build by ourselves. It requires at least one other person (child, spouse or friend) or a community (church congregation or professional network) of others who will live beyond our death. Someone else has to continue to live on to know our story, and in knowing our story, it becomes meaningful.

So if you ever want to immediately remember what symbolic immortality is all about, let us leave you with some lyrics penned by American rapper Macklemore in his song, *Glorious*:

> *I heard you die twice, once when they bury you in the grave*
> *And the second time is the last time that somebody mentions your name*

So when I leave here on this earth, did I take more than I gave?
Did I look out for the people or did I do it all for fame?

A gift in your will to charity is one way that a donor can engage in a second stage death defence by invoking symbolic immortality.

Let us circle back to the *2019 State Of The Legacy Nation* research results for a moment.

We know that 7% of Canadians have left a gift in their will and 30% of direct mail donors have. Might it be that direct mail donors share your charity's values, are do-gooders, and giving is an extension of themselves? In this way, these folks are already primed for creative symbolic immortality.

So, what can you do with all this new information? Well, it sheds a whole new light on why we should focus our legacy efforts on the 60+ donor. It's not just about their age, and it's not about the fact that, practically speaking, the time to realization is much shorter for the organization.

It's about their life stage. Your legacy donor is in the third act of life. They have grappled with, and come to terms with, their own mortality. They're seeking ways to extend their lives so that something of them remains long after they're gone. These donors couldn't be more primed to talk about a gift in a will — but you need to use symbolic immortality and autobiography in your communication strategies to get them there.

PIONEER THINKERS

So, we know that a legacy gift comes from the part of the brain that deals with who you are, why you're here, and what you'll leave behind. But those are big existential questions, without easy answers. How can you possibly weave them into your legacy marketing?

There were three contemporary pioneering thinkers from the 20th century whose framing of existential questions and answers is still useful in understanding the brain that makes bequests. Let's look at each of these thinkers briefly in turn.

Victor Frankl (1905 – 1997)

Victor Frankl was an Austrian neurologist and psychologist who had the misfortune to be of Jewish descent during WW2. Frankl and his entire family were interned in Nazi concentration camps and only he and one of his sisters survived.

While he was imprisoned, Frankl theorized that those prisoners who survived the horrors of the Holocaust best were those with a strong purpose to their lives – often, something meaningful to do or someone important to reconnect with after the war.

Frankl developed a theory called 'Logotherapy' which became known as 'The Third School of Viennese Psychiatry.' Frankl made the case that our primary drive as humans is to find purpose and meaning in life. Citing his own wartime existence, he believed he survived the Holocaust because of his burning desire to write his book *Man's Search for Meaning* and to reunite with his wife (who died in the camps).

In all of our work over more than three decades, we Good Workers have always found that donors derive a great sense of satisfaction from their giving precisely because their philanthropy makes their lives feel more purposeful and meaningful. Speaking specifically about meaning and purpose with your legacy prospects is a great way to get them into the right 'mental zone' to consider – and make – a bequest to you.

Erik Erikson (1902 – 1994)

Erik Erikson was a German/American developmental psychologist and psychoanalyst who, like Victor Frankl, studied under Sigmund Freud in Vienna before WW2. Being part Jewish, Frankl left Austria for Denmark, and later attended brand-name universities in the USA such as Harvard and Yale.

While Frankl was focused on the search for meaning, Erikson believed that the human identity (ego) evolves through eight stages during our lifetimes. The purpose of the life journey, according to Erikson, is to successfully navigate each of the stages in order to progress to the next in a healthy and promising way. For example, babies seek to feel safe, while toddlers strive to step out and discover their independent selves.

Two of Erikson's stages resonate with us as planned giving fundraisers in a big way:

- In our seventh stage (aged about 40-65), we develop a capacity – even a need – for what he calls *'generativity'*. As Erikson defines it, generativity is a desire to both have a deep concern for people other than ourselves (often developed as we become parents) and to nurture, teach, and support younger members of generations that follow us. If you've ever heard the old saying about *'planting a tree in whose shade you will never sit,'* that's generativity in a nutshell.

- In our last stage of life (roughly aged 60+) we reach a fork in life's road where we either find ourselves on the path of ego integrity or the path of despair. As you can imagine, the path of despair is one of deep regret for choices made during life and the painful consequences that those choices have rendered. On the other hand, ego integrity is the process of reaching a place where one is satisfied with life and with self, and for the most part joyful at the path just taken.

It's a no-brainer that you would create legacy content that speaks specifically to these experiences, in order to light up that part of the prospect's brain.

Abraham Maslow (1908 – 1970)

While you may or may not have heard of Victor Frankl and Erik Erikson, you have probably heard about Maslow's Hierarchy of Needs. Some of us studied it in high school, or perhaps others during a Psychology 101 course at university. Maslow was born to Ukrainian-Jewish immigrant parents in New York City, and later became an academic at Columbia and Brandeis Universities.

Maslow created a five-level hierarchy of human existence. In his hierarchy, a person must achieve and maintain a level before they can rise to the next level up. So, one can only achieve the fifth level when the first four are firmly in place. To Maslow, life's journey was the navigation of this hierarchy and the search for the top level.

What is most interesting to us is that we can talk about each of these five levels when we talk about legacy giving. The first two levels are more outward-looking, in that they focus more on the recipient of the philanthropic gift than on the donor:

- The legacy gift could help provide the most basic **physiological** needs, like food, water, warmth, and perhaps, by extension, health care.

- A donor's bequest might also provide **safety**-oriented benefits to recipients like family, health, employment, housing, and so on.

If we were framing legacy messaging for bequest prospects, we would tend to frame the next three levels of Maslow's hierarchy more in terms of the legacy donor:

- **Love** and **belonging** can actually be framed both looking outward at the recipient of the gift *and* inward at the person making the gift. We can talk about how a bequest to a charity will show the recipient love and help them belong in their family or community. We can – and should! – talk about the tremendous love that goes into making a gift in a will. In fact, we like to suggest to the prospect that making legacy gifts is one of the most noble acts of the human experience, and that these gifts are examples of humanity at its highest order.

- Next, we seek to attain the level of **esteem** and **respect.** According to Maslow, it's incredibly important to us as humans that we develop strong self-esteem and self-respect. Leaving a bequest is certainly one way to contribute to these needs, and you can incorporate this messaging when speaking with legacy prospects. As humans, we also highly value the esteem and respect of others. We are, after all, the most social animals on the planet, and the approval and acceptance of the group is critical to the health and survival of the individual.

- Finally, Maslow talks about **self-actualization** as the highest rung on his ladder of human needs. While self-actualization might manifest itself in creativity, intellectualization, and achievement, it can also be found in the areas of moral superiority, a strong ethical code, and humanistic beliefs. It is in this latter group that the legacy gift clearly fits – and we think that fundraisers should speak explicitly about these ideas to legacy prospects.

While Frankl, Erikson, and Maslow all have quite different emphases in their understandings of the human psyche and the life journey, they also share some very compelling similarities. They all take a very existential view in their work – in other words, they consider the question *'Why am I here?'* to be the most fundamental of all life's mysteries. They all acknowledge our evolution as a highly social species. They all weave morals and ethics – in some way, shape, or form – as they try to define what constitutes *'the good life'*.

This can be helpful to you in crafting narratives that will speak to symbolic immortality.

SUMMING UP THE GIVING BRAIN

We know that we've thrown a lot of new information at you in this chapter – and perhaps it's been a little overwhelming for you to try to absorb it all. That's ok.

It might help you to see this chapter as being akin to the foundation of a building. Once the building is built, you can't see it – but without the foundation, the building wouldn't stand. Concepts like the triune brain model, the autobiographical centre of the brain, and life's third act are the foundational ideas upon which some of the tools we'll soon show you are based.

We don't just want you to do your legacy fundraising right. We want you to understand *why* it's right. Because in our opinion, the most important element of being a great fundraiser is having a deep understanding of your donors and prospects. Once you have absorbed the ideas and concepts from this chapter, you'll have come a long way in understanding the legacy donors that will soon be yours!

CHAPTER 6:
STORYTELLING FOR A LEGACY AUDIENCE

So, now you understand the brain of a legacy donor – what makes them tick, what they need to hear from you, and how they make the jump to a gift. Now it's time to start actually reaching out and communicating with your prospects in a compelling, relevant, and persuasive way.

This chapter will offer you some practical advice on what we know legacy persuasion best practice to be.

THE FUTURE BELONGS TO THE BEST STORYTELLER

When Russell James wanted to see what happens in a donor's brain when they make a gift in their will, he used fMRI to take a literal look inside the donor's mind. Guess what? That same technology has shown us what a powerful tool stories are in teaching, entertaining, informing, and *persuading* audiences of all types.

Look at the two brain images below. These show us vividly how much more engaged we become when we're listening to a story as opposed to looking at a chart or graph.

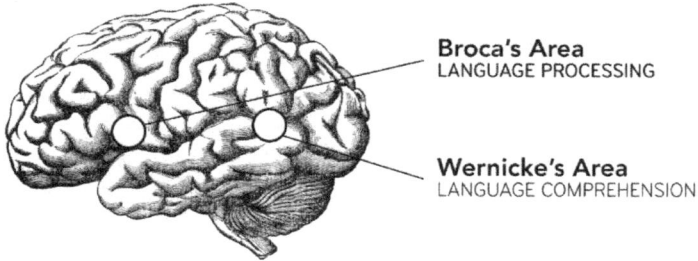

Broca's Area
LANGUAGE PROCESSING

Wernicke's Area
LANGUAGE COMPREHENSION

Your Brain on Data

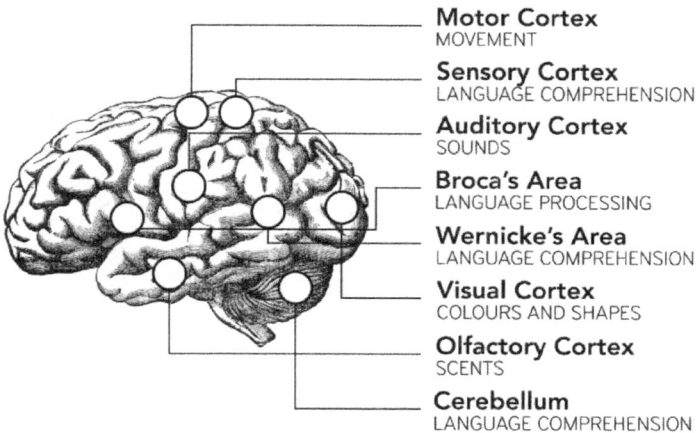

Motor Cortex
MOVEMENT

Sensory Cortex
LANGUAGE COMPREHENSION

Auditory Cortex
SOUNDS

Broca's Area
LANGUAGE PROCESSING

Wernicke's Area
LANGUAGE COMPREHENSION

Visual Cortex
COLOURS AND SHAPES

Olfactory Cortex
SCENTS

Cerebellum
LANGUAGE COMPREHENSION

Your Brain on Stories

Stories engage us on our most primal levels. They can make us experience all of our five senses. They can trigger powerful memories of the past and dreams of the future. They can fire up both those primary emotions and our reptilian instinct to survive.

Most compelling of all is the ability of a well-told story to suspend our disbelief. When our brains do this, we stop being a passive witness to a story and we become a living, breathing character in it. If the right person is telling the right story to the right person, the audience member's story and the storyteller's story become one and the same. My story becomes your story. My legacy gift becomes your legacy gift. You go (in your imagination) from being a bystander to being a legacy-maker.

Put another way, stories are where we marry the empathic brain (the mammalian brain that manages the giving impulse) and the autobiographical brain (where legacy gifts truly come from). By choosing the right story and storyteller to speak to the autobiographical brain, and telling that story in such a way that we can activate the empathic brain, we're truly able to get the donor to take a walk in the shoes of someone who has made this kind of commitment and obtained this kind of symbolic immortality. And when they take that walk – when they see someone else has lived a life very similar to theirs, and will continue to live on in this way – it becomes a very persuasive idea indeed.

In other words, storytelling is the absolute heart of legacy marketing. The marriage of heart and soul. The invitation on a personal journey. The promise of a life that lasts far beyond this mortal coil.

This is powerful stuff – and it's beautiful stuff. Legacy storytelling is the reason we Good Workers love this work beyond measure!

THE MARRIAGE PROPOSAL ROLE-PLAY

When Fraser does legacy giving workshops at fundraising conferences, he loves to recruit four volunteers from the audience and do a marriage proposal exercise. Fraser divides them into two couples – in each couple, one person is about to propose marriage to the other.

Fraser asks the first proposer to construct their marriage proposal from a financial and accounting point of view. He then asks the second proposer to construct his proposal as if he were a romantic poet.

Their proposals often sound something like this:

Accountant: *"Jenny, I've stayed up late the last couple of nights working on some spreadsheets. And you know what? I think it could make a lot of sense for you and I to form a marital partnership. If you sold your condo and we applied the net to my house, we could have my mortgage paid off in just seven years. Assuming that we earn cost of living salary increases that equal inflation, I think we can afford to save for post-secondary education for two children. By combining our grocery spending – not to mention utilities – we could put almost $6,000 more into our RRSP accounts. So, Jenny, I see lots of upside to us doing this before New Year's (so that I can claim the spousal tax credit). What do you say? Should we move forward on this?"*

Poet: *"Jenny, when I awake in the morning with your warm, even breath on the back of my neck, I know the feeling of life itself. When I look into your eyes, I see the sky and the ocean. I see your heart and your soul. I see my future and my life's purpose. Jenny, I want to spend every day of the rest of my life with you. I want to raise children with you and share in every journey your life takes you on. You make me feel fully alive. You bring out my best self. I can't imagine a future without you in it. Jenny, would you do me the ultimate honour of agreeing to be my wife?"*

Which proposal would *you* rather receive? We're guessing it's the latter.

This the perfect example of the importance of 'why' instead of 'how' that is absolutely vital to legacy storytelling. It's the importance of evoking emotions, rather than making cases for tax breaks. The role of the mammal brain to overrule the big brain.

When we go the numbers route, it turns us off. It feels cold and clinical and complicated. And that becomes more true the older we get. Our ability to comprehend numbers decreases with age, but our ability to understands words never does.

When we go the emotional route, it sucks us in. It's evocative. It's instinctual. As you read about Jenny, you see your own partner in your mind's eye. If you've been married, you might even have reminisced on your own engagement. And not just that, you probably thought about your own wedding day, your first anniversary, your fifth, your 25th. Maybe you visualized your 50th anniversary, even though it's a ways away.

In a hundred words, you saw your entire life in the blink of an eye. That's the true power of a story: to connect the donor's life to the storyteller's life, to find their common values and experiences. And then, to show (not tell!) how someone with such a similar life has attained all-important symbolic immortality, through a gift in their will.

STICK WITH WHAT WORKS!

Now that we've laid out some context, let's go to a list of very practical and effective ways to communicate legacy messages with your bequest prospects. Here are six ideas to get you started:

1. Speak to the Autobiographical Brain

The autobiographical brain is preoccupied with key questions about who we are and how we've lived our lives. For you as a legacy fundraiser, there's only really one question that matters: *'How will I be remembered when I'm gone?'*

Telling an autobiographical story will help the donor answer that question. And the answer, in this case, is by making a gift in their will to your organization – a gift that will speak to symbolic immortality.

It's helpful to think of your subject's life story like a book. It follows, chapter by chapter, in chronological order. The story literally begins at birth, goes through childhood and adulthood, and passes into life's third act – where you find your donor now.

And throughout that person's life, your organization's mission, work, and values (if not the organization specifically) should be a consistent theme. Perhaps at the tender age of 10, your parents took you to see the *Phantom of the Opera* at the Princess of Wales Theatre in Toronto, and you fell in love with theatre. Throughout your high school years, you adored drama class – you were even cast as Maria in *West Side Story* in your senior year! In university, you used to wait at the box office on Friday night for cheap student tickets. And, once you were a little better established, a membership to the National Arts Centre became a permanent line item in your budget. Quite simply, theatre has always been a part of your life. It's become a part of *you*. So it felt very natural to include a gift in your will to your favourite theatre, because just like your family and friends, it's been a meaningful part of life for what feels like forever.

This evocation of experiences and values that are likely shared with your donors help bring them closer to you. It makes them reflect on how their lifelong support of your work has become a part of their own story and their own self. Sure, their first show was *Cats* instead of *Phantom*, and maybe they never took to the stage themselves – but the parallels are all there.

So a gift in your will acts as an extension of this lifelong relationship between your donors and a cause that they don't just care about, but that has shaped them in some way. Think of it as the epilogue of the book – that one last chapter that happens after the person passes from this world. And to circle back to Dr. Russell James's work again, this is where the donor is mentally completing the final chapter of their visualized autobiography in the future.

2. Press Emotional Buttons

You'll recall that our eight emotional pairings – the ones on which all others are based – are fear, anger, sadness, joy, trust, disgust, surprise, and anticipation.

If you really want your legacy messages to resonate, then your best bet is to make members of your audience *feel* something. The late playwright, poet and civil rights activist Maya Angelou once said:

> *"You'll forget what I say. You'll forget what I do. But, you'll never forget how I make you feel."*

So, think about your messenger. Think about your audience member. Think about your cause and mission. And, think about the emotions that are most powerful and appropriate to your own particular situation. Once you've identified the emotion you want to ignite, don't be afraid to do it! Be brave. Step courageously out from behind your charts and graphs and show lots of heart. Your prospects will reward you for it.

3. The Most Persuasive Voice

When you're looking to communicate the legacy giving story to your bequest prospects, the most persuasive voice you can use is not your Executive Director, your Board chair, or even a celebrity spokesperson.

Instead, the best storyteller is someone whose own life and experiences most closely mirror those of your prospect. This enables you to more easily activate the autobiographical brain in your writing, because the connections are all there for the taking.

Think of it this way: Jacqueline is a widowed woman in her 70s who has kids and grandkids and cares about cancer. If you really want to persuade Jacqueline to make a bequest, have your storyteller be a woman in her 70s who has kids and grandkids and who has had her own experience with cancer. When Jacqueline hears how this woman has made a bequest, she'll be more inclined to imagine herself doing the same.

There are seven primary storytellers you can use to tell an autobiographical story:

- Living bequest donor: According to Russell James's research, the most effective (and most persuasive) storyteller is a donor who has made his or her own legacy gift. We knew this intuitively before we read James's research, and we're grateful to him for his research rigour. We see the living donor testimonial story this way: When it's done well, it's like holding a mirror up in the face of the prospect you're speaking to. That example of Jacqueline above? That's a living donor testimonial at work.

- Spouse of the deceased: Many individuals who leave a gift in their will are widows (the female surviving spouse with or without children), and more rarely widowers (since women typically outlive men). When a widow/er thinks about their legacy, it includes their husband or wife; it's a legacy of two people. All of their assets, and the life they have led, is something they built together. So when a widow is the storyteller, it sparks joy to speak about their spouse, to say their name, and to maintain their legacy. The gift in their will is one of remembrance, or one they planned to leave together after both of their deaths. Russell James's research showed, counter to any best practice at the time, that individuals responded to messages about charitable bequests that were made in honour or in tribute. This makes sense to us, because we've long known that widows have a powerful autobiographical narrative that is strongly tied to creative symbolic immortality.

- Visionary/leader: This could be your Executive Director, a long-standing Board member, or a similar executive role – especially if they have a long tenure with your organization and are well-known with your donors. This storyteller works because it's a careful balancing act of the past (the storyteller's life story and what brought them to be involved with your organization) and the future (the world they envision and are working towards every day). This can be a great tool for effectively communicating future need and helping the donor understand what their gift will be accomplishing in 20 or 30 years. Of course, this storyteller works best if they've left a gift in their will, too. They can't only see the vision – they need to be a part of it.

- Founder: Much like our living bequester tells the story of their life, the founder can tell the story of the organization's life, interwoven with their own personal story. This creates the sense of a living, breathing organization with a lasting legacy of its own that the donor can become a part of through their gift.

- Beneficiary of planned gift: Another way to demonstrate impact, this storyteller shows the donor their own symbolic immortality in action – or at least, how it could look. This brings the impact to life in a very real way. It walks the walk. If your beneficiary is also a living legacy donor, you've hit the jackpot. Otherwise, it can be challenging to create the experiential connections required to really evoke the autobiographical brain.

- Family of the deceased: The living relatives of your donor, particularly children, provide social proof that you can take care of your children and grandchildren and still give to charity. Having a family member tell a donor's life story speaks back to both biologic and creative symbolic immortality. It can demonstrate how a person lives on through relatives who know their story, share it, and keep it alive. It's also about the donor's own self living on through the gift and the charitable good deeds it enables. Despite this strong connection to symbolic immortality, we have found that when the living relative is someone other than the children the story isn't nearly as effective in identifying prospects, suspects, and expectancies. Perhaps this is because death is front and centre in this narrative.

- Deceased bequest donor: This is where we simply tell the life story of a deceased donor. It's a third person perspective on the individual, their life, accomplishments, and achievements. This is the type of story that you'll most typically find in a legacy newsletter.

In your legacy marketing, you want to use a mix of these storytellers (and we'll talk about how you can use them later!). But the key thing to keep in mind – no matter which storyteller you use – is to choose people who will closely reflect the life of the prospect in as many ways as possible, and whose journey to symbolic immortality will resonate deeply with them.

4. Preempt Objections

When we Good Workers do focus groups with annual donors and begin asking them about charitable bequests, they get quite excited and enthusiastic. But, at some point, somebody sticks a pin in the feel-good balloon. Well, two pins actually.

In the business world, salespeople talk about 'removing customer objections.' These are the things customers say when they like a product but then say something starting with 'but.' Like, *'but it's awfully expensive,'* or *'I don't like the colour,'* or *'I need to check with my spouse.'* The best salespeople on the planet are the ones who can convince their customers to overcome their objections and buy the product.

So, let's look at the two most common 'sales objections' in the field of legacy giving, and how you can use the right storyteller to get around them:

Common Objection #1 – "But What About My Family?"

The first way that donors put the brakes on their enthusiasm is to remind themselves that they have family obligations to fulfill. This usually takes the form of spouses, kids, and/or grandkids. After all, the latter two are your prospect's biological symbolic immortality – they *must* be provided for.

There are two ways to deal with this objection – one persuasive, one practical. We like to use both in different ways, depending on the tactic at hand.

Persuasively, the best way to circumvent the family obligation barrier is to let the donor know that not only can they do both, but they likely have enough money to do so. The caveat here is that you, the organization, cannot deliver this message! It would be far too self-serving.

Instead, use a living bequester testimonial to hold up that mirror and have another legacy donor communicate the message. If Jacqueline tells her story, and says that she has children and grandchildren, but still found room in her estate to make a gift, you've shown your prospect that perhaps she can do both too.

From a practical perspective, let donors know about residual gifts. This giving structure, which fulfills all your obligations and leaves the remainder to charity, can feel very reassuring indeed to a donor who isn't sure about the size of their estate, but knows they have important needs that must be met.

Common Objection #2: "But I'm Not Rich."

The second way that prospects pull back is when they start to think that legacy giving is something that only rich people do. They might have the idea that bequests are the territory of wealthy philanthropists, and not middle-class donors. This view is more common among elderly prospects in our experience.

When the widow of McDonald's founder Ray Kroc died, her bequest of $1.5 billion to the Salvation Army made headlines around the world. When a retired schoolteacher who lives around the corner leaves $38,000 to his community hospital, it tends not to get much fanfare.

So, when we did some work with an international development organization in the U.S., one of our first letters was from a retired Boston bus driver. In very simple and ordinary language, he talked about his blue-collar life, his values, and his religious faith. We feel that using 'everyman' testimonials is the best way to have your prospects feel, *"I can do this too!"*

This also means that when you use an Executive storyteller, try to downplay as much as possible their wealth and status. Sure, your storyteller might be a high-powered stockbroker on Bay Street, but focus instead on the care his mother received at your hospital before she passed away. Focus on the connection to the cause – never the size of the gift.

5. Writing for the 50+ Brain

It shouldn't come as a surprise that your brain changes as you age. The 50+ brain is quite different in how it understands, perceives, and experiences the world. We become more right-brained as we age.

You're probably familiar with thinking about the brain as two separate hemispheres – right and left. It's often said that the left-brain has a more a distinctive analytic and verbal style of thinking while the right-brain has a more holistic and creative style. It turns out that both hemispheres of the brain work together and we use both of them all the time. So modern neuroscience has debunked some of our myths about right and left brain functioning.

But as we age, we tend to experience an increase in right brain participation in our mental functions. This leads to changes in communications preferences. The right hemisphere is emotional and intuitive, and is less interested in details than in the total picture. It also tends to perceive reality in images — in sensory images to be more precise.

Dr. Kara D. Federmeier is a cognitive neuroscientist whose research focuses on language, memory, and hemispheric asymmetries throughout the lifespan. She undertook an experiment where she used different adjectives ('green' and 'interesting') to change the meaning of the same noun ('book') because the brain processes concrete and abstract words differently. Where 'green book' is easy to picture this in your mind, 'interesting book' causes you to think about the content of the book and not the physical book, which makes it more abstract.

In this particular study, she was surprised to find that the *right* hemisphere conjured imagery-related brain activity to 'green book' when compared to 'interesting book'. While the left hemisphere is important for language processing, it would seem that the right hemisphere plays a special role in creating the rich sensory experience that often accompanies language comprehension. It's what makes reading books or letters so pleasurable.

Since the right hemisphere perceives reality in images, you need to be very specific, concrete, and metaphorical in your word choice to paint the picture in a donor's mind with the intention of creating sensory images. Here's a story.

> *One day, David mistakenly ate a peanut butter cracker at a friend's house and died from anaphylactic shock.*

Now, let's rewrite this same story for the 50+ donor.

> *One day, David stumbled home after mistakenly eating a peanut butter cracker at a friend's house. This was 1980, before I even knew EpiPens existed. By the time the ambulance arrived, his lips and ears were purple.*

Writing more sensual and emotional copy is a particularly salient finding for fundraisers. You need to be concrete and specific, not abstract, when writing your copy so that you can create that sensory experience that pulls on the mammalian brain and takes your donor back to their autobiographical mindset.

6. Civics Versus Boomers

Given that Civics and Boomers combined account for 83% of all legacy gifts, you want to target your messaging here. When it comes to communicating persuasively with Civics and Boomers, there are some great similarities between these cohorts – and yet, there are profound differences.

Here are three simple and practical tips to get you started reaching both these audiences effectively in your legacy gift marketing program:

- **Start with their similarities.** Both groups have entered their 'third act' of life. Their kids are raised and educations are paid for. They own their homes mortgage-free (this is where the gift money comes from!). They are becoming more introspective and existential in their thinking. They want their lives to have meaning and purpose – and they want to feel that their lives have been worthwhile, to others as well as themselves. After age 60, we tend to think more with our autobiographical brains when we consider bequests – so creating a coherent story of one's life becomes an essential ingredient in creating your persuasive messages.

- **Talk to Civics about responsibility and duty.** Keep in mind that this generation came of age during the Great Depression of the 1930s, WW2 in the 1940s, and the Cold War of the 1950s. This group places a high priority on safety and security, and comes from a 'wartime effort' notion of collective duty and responsibility. This is the generation of Frank Sinatra, of black-and-white movies starring Humphrey Bogart. They are savers – and they value material security over new experiences and adventure.

  If you knew you were writing legacy copy for an entirely Civic audience, you would talk about the idea of conforming to society's idea of the model citizen – and you would frame the bequest as an opportunity to 'make the grade' as a good person and citizen. You might use words like 'responsibility', 'duty', 'obligation', and 'respect' as key parts of the messaging.

- **Talk to Boomers about identity and being special.** Boomers are a very different breed of cat from their Civic parents. This group came of age with the Beatles appearing on Ed Sullivan, the first moon landing, Woodstock, the Civil Rights Movement, and the Vietnam War. Unlike their conformist parents, Boomers felt the need to break away from the established rules and do what feels right. Boomers – unlike their Civic parents – also grew up with a healthy distrust of authority. Boomers feel like they were born to make a difference. And as they age, they can still flex their 'change the world' muscles (because they have most of the wealth today!).

If you knew you were creating content for a Boomer audience, you would take a different approach. You would talk about how a legacy gift can lift the individual donor above the crowd and make her stand out as a truly special person. You might use words and phrases like 'first', 'best', 'leader', 'set an example', and 'achievement'.

While there are real and profound differences between Civics and Boomers, their passage into their third act of life is their unifying bond. When you speak to this third act, you'll be off to a great start with both groups and well on your way to triggering bequest decisions.

THE GOOD WORKS GOLDEN RULE

Over the years, we have honed a best practice that we believe presents the case for legacy giving in the most powerful and persuasive way possible. We call it (immodestly, we admit!) our Golden Rule, and we use it in every single legacy touchpoint we craft for clients.

Our rule follows a simple numerical formula that goes like this: 40-30-20-10. Here's how it works:

- **40% of your message content should be about the donor.** This can be created in either of two ways. It can be about the prospect and her life – or it can be a testimonial from a legacy gift donor. Either way, almost half of what you say is about the person who's made a legacy gift or who might make a legacy gift. If you're now thinking about the autobiographical brain, you're bang on!

- **30% of your message content should be about your cause.** Now, don't go jumping the gun here – your cause is not your organization, and it's not your mission. Not yet! If you're a hospital foundation, your cause is health. If you're a university, your cause is higher education. If you're a social service agency, your cause is the alleviation of poverty. If you're a humane society, your cause is animal welfare. Take it from us: donors care because of the cause, and they give to your organization so that they can do something about this cause that they care so deeply about.

- *Now* – and only now – can you talk about yourself! At this point, you can allocate about **20% of your message content to talking about your organization and its mission.** Please don't go over the 20% rule – and trust us, it will be hard to do at first. Your Executive Director and Board members will probably feel *very* itchy that you're not promoting your organization's brand more explicitly. Now is the time when you have to take a stand for your donor. Stick to your guns and create messages that will make prospects give rather than make Board Members stop griping.

- And, last but not least, you can spend up to **10% of your message content actually talking about the gift**. Yes, now you can mention (but only mention) the money. Because, the legacy gift isn't about money at all. It's about beliefs and values. It's about life and heart and soul. It's about becoming the most loving and evolved kind of human being. To link the legacy gift too closely to money is to cheapen and disrespect it – and none of us want to do that!

A LITTLE SIDEBAR:
THE LEGACY GENERATION GAP

One of our fundraising colleagues and friends (and Fraser's daughter) is a woman named Rory Green who works in planned giving at a Canadian university. As we're writing this book, Rory has just celebrated her 30th birthday.

As a planned giving fundraiser, Rory is talking every day with prospects and donors who are in their 70s and 80s. These people are 40 or 50 (or more!) years older than Rory. They grew up in a different time. Their cultural references and milestones are totally different. While Rory is a new mom, these donors have been grandparents for a long time. While Rory is still in a relatively early stage of her career, her donors have been retired for years.

There are huge differences between Rory's life and the lives of the audience she's connecting with. If she wants to be successful at her job – and advance her institution's mission – she needs to learn what it's like to be old!

In all our years of building our expertise in the area of legacy gift persuasion, we have come to the consensus that one obstacle above all others stands in the way of success. That obstacle is the almost inevitable generation gap (or more accurately, to follow Jane Fonda's metaphor, the Act Gap) that exists between legacy fundraisers on the one hand and legacy prospects and donors on the other hand.

To put it in its most simple terms: The vast majority of planned giving fundraisers are in their second act of life (between ages 30 and 60), while the vast majority of their prospects and donors are in their final act at age 60+. The legacy fundraiser needs to see the world through her prospect's eyes, because that prospect isn't going to think like a 40-year-old again just to make it easy for you.

The big skill you need to acquire – and one of the principle lessons that this book is setting out to teach you – is this: *In order to do really great legacy fundraising work, you need to learn to think, feel, and see like someone who is one or two generations older than you.*

CHAPTER 7:
THE LEGACY FACTORY:
TACTICS AND TOOLS

So, you've done your foundational work.

You have a good understanding of the legacy marketplace. You're developing a good feel for the legacy audience and what makes them tick. You understand what motivates someone to leave a gift in their will. And, you've laid out a singular strategy, with input from the right stakeholders in your organization.

Now, it's time to figure out how to actually implement that strategy! In this chapter, we'll lay out the tools and tactics that we've used time and time again to market legacy giving successfully.

THE LEGACY CULTIVATION CYCLE

In Chapter 3, we talked about creating a legacy program and not a one-off campaign. The rationale here is that by creating a full program that drips legacy messages into donor minds over a long period of time, you're respecting that the legacy decision can take months to make – and making sure you'll be on the radar when the donor is next updating their will.

Ultimately, your program should be designed to do two things. First, it persuades prospects to consider, commit to, and include a gift in their will. Second, it stewards those confirmed expectancies to deepen the commitment to you and, with a little luck and lot of persistence, get them to increase the size of their gift.

We often call the journey that leads to realizing each of these objectives the *legacy cultivation cycle*. From a tactical perspective, we want you to think of it as your legacy factory.

This factory is packed floor-to-ceiling with conveyor belts. Each belt moves donors who are at a specific place in the bequest decision-making process, further along in that process.

So, if you visualize your factory, there is an expectancy conveyor belt carrying donors who have let you know they've included your organization in their will. This belt is a never-ending loop. Donors never come off it, but instead are consistently stewarded up with gratitude and impact messaging.

That belt is preceded by one that carries your prospect group – the folks who are very close to achieving that first objective, but who aren't quite there yet. This group is receiving messages designed to persuade them to take the next step, commit to the bequest, and let you know about it.

Your prospect belt is fed by two more belts. One is carrying your suspect group, who haven't outright said no to a legacy gift, but aren't yet warm enough to be considered a full prospect. They're receiving replicas of the prospect messages at a lower frequency. The other belt is carrying new, qualified prospects, selected because of their demonstrated loyalty to your charity. They should receive two or three years' worth of active marketing before you move them to other belts as warranted.

And last but certainly not least, yet another belt is carrying the 'not interested' donors out of your legacy factory and off to your monthly, mid-level, and major gifts factories. These are folks who aren't interested in hearing more about this way of giving, or they're folks who have already left a gift in their will to charity but you're not one of the charities listed.

But the belts don't simply move one group to another in sequence. That's far too simple an analogy for such a complex, personal gift. The belts connect with each other. They split off from each other. They move at different speeds. Most importantly, they have loops and turns that can bring a person back to the beginning of a given belt. So, a prospect who is coming close to the end of the belt, but still hasn't confirmed a gift, doesn't just get kicked out of the factory for not giving on your schedule. Instead, they're carried back to the start of that prospect belt, over and over, for as long as they need.

This factory enables you to apply mass marketing theories to the incredibly personal legacy journey of a single person. We like that this metaphor speaks to the fact that legacy marketing doesn't end with a confirmation of a gift. That simply means the stewardship work must now begin! And, we like that it helps illustrate the ongoing nature of legacy marketing – that touchpoints can be reused over and over, with new prospects and existing ones.

But there is one caveat, and it's this: Just because you're mapping your program as if it were a factory, it absolutely does NOT mean you should envision legacy giving as being in any way transactional. What we want you to take from the factory metaphor is the sense of movement – both sequentially, from one phase to the next, and cyclically, where a prospect might need to go through a certain part more than once – that is so vital to planning and building your legacy program.

This chapter will give you what you need to map out your legacy cultivation cycle, along with ideas about how to steward those confirmed expectancies and grow their commitment to you.

The prospect and suspect belts (mostly the former) are where the majority of the heavy lifting is done on your part, usually over a 24- to 36-month period. That's where you're doing all the persuasive work – picking the right storytellers to tell the right stories to trigger the right emotions and memories in your donor's brain.

So, let's start there, with the tactics that we've seen best persuade prospects to become fully-fledged legacy donors. We'll talk more about how to segment your prospects later on in this chapter.

DIRECT MAIL

Think back to your high-quality legacy prospect, as we discussed in Chapter 2. What do we know about them? Well, they're a long-time donor (not necessarily a high-value donor) who is deeply connected to your cause. They're aged 60+, so they've likely already confronted their mortality and have got some financial stability. And most of their giving happens through the mail. Remember that 30% of direct mail donors have left a gift in their will in comparison to 7% of those who don't give through the mail.

That is why it makes so much sense for direct mail to be the cornerstone of your legacy marketing program. It's a tactic with which your audience is not only familiar, but to which they've proven responsive. By focusing your efforts on direct mail, you're speaking to your audience in the language that *they* choose and amping up the all-important relevance factor.

We also know from extensive focus group work with donors that the majority of your legacy prospects don't want the perceived pressure of a personal visit or a phone call. On the other hand, they quite like the idea of having a package of materials on the dining room table that they can read and consider at their own pace. While it's a great practice to let your prospects know that you're available for visits and personal conversations, you should never push for them. That, to most donors, is crossing the aggressiveness line.

Planning Your Direct Mail Cycle
At the outset, you'll want to plan your full cycle of mailings over 24- to 36-months. Generally, our legacy mailing series include three to six touchpoints through the mail aligned with your strategy and program maturity.

Ideally, you'll aim to send a legacy direct mail package every few months, working around your regular mailing schedule. January often works because the new year can propel us into a space of reflection. Spring, too, is often a prime time, and you can use the timeliness to evoke relevant themes – new life, re-birth, planting seeds, and so forth – as a bonus. Summer can be a great time to send legacy mail, when there tends to be a natural lull in annual giving programs. Fall works as snowbirds may update their wills before escaping the long, cold, and snowy Canadian winter.

**ANNUAL GIVING AND LEGACY GIVING:
A MATCH MADE IN HEAVEN**

Whatever you do, please don't pull out your legacy donors from the annual giving stream! While it might feel like a lot of touchpoints to you, it won't feel the same way to your donor, because legacy mailings won't feel like a solicitation (if they're done right). In fact, legacy mailings tend to have a positive effect on annual giving revenue. We typically see them lift response to the next direct mail piece the prospect receives. Furthermore, once someone makes the commitment and includes you in their will, they usually increase the size of their annual gifts to you – permanently!

Each mailing in your series should come from a unique storyteller who is able to share their own personal journey to leaving a gift in their will to your organization. Ultimately, each will very softly and tactfully ask donors if they might consider giving in this way themselves – and you'll include a reply coupon that invites donors to share their thoughts about a gift in a will.

We suggest you start by envisioning the stories you want to tell over that two-year period. Now, these don't have to be stories you know you have already! We love to start this process by envisioning our dream story sequence, one that we believe will hit every key emotional trigger for your donors. Then, we go out and find the stories we need, or tweak the sequence as needed.

But let's not get ahead of ourselves. As you're crafting this ideal story sequence (we call it a story inventory), ask yourself some key questions: What do your donors value? What matters to them? What is it about *your* organization's work that makes your legacy prospects tick? How can you align with their autobiography and need for symbolic immortality?

For a health charity, it might be the power of research to find a cure for Alzheimer's, because almost all of your donors have been personally impacted by the disease. If you work in animal welfare, it might be the need to find forever homes for cats and dogs – the thought of an innocent animal suffering upsets your donor deeply. For a university, perhaps your donor values education and only had the chance to go and unlock the career and life they've led because of a scholarship they received from your institution.

Really dig into what has kept these folks giving to you year after year after year. Then, find ways to extrapolate that connection and link it up with the future need. Why will you need legacy gift money in the future, and how will it further the goals and motivations your donor has already demonstrated with their loyal, long-time giving? This is the place where you'll marry organizational vision with donor values to create an exceptionally appealing offer.

Once you've identified your donor values and connected them to the impact they can have 20 or 30 years down the line, start to think about how you can weave the two together into compelling narratives. For that health charity, maybe you want to be able to tell the story of a researcher whose work is funded by legacy gifts and the breakthroughs this has enabled. The university might want to feature a student whose tuition is paid for by legacy donors (bonus points if that student is studying something relevant to your donor's values!).

Next, consider the right order for all the stories in your inventory. Think about how the series will build upon itself and be experienced holistically by the donor. How can each storyteller address common objections to leaving a gift in their will (recall those are "*What about my family?*" and "*I'm not rich*")? Perhaps you intentionally include donors who have children, to demonstrate that one can leave a gift to charity in a will and provide for loved ones.

You'll also want to consider how each story and storyteller can frame your mission in a unique way. How can each letter talk about future need and the impact of a gift in your will differently? Pick and sequence stories that will approach your mission and vision from different places. For example, an international development charity who knows their donors value clean water *and* education for girls might have one letter from a successful businesswoman who got an education because her school was built with legacy donor dollars and now she's decided to make the same gift in her will. Then, have another letter from a lifelong volunteer who has built dozens of wells and has included a gift in their will to build even more after they're gone.

If you're intentional in your story selection, you can make sure that your donors have a well-rounded perspective of legacy giving and all that it can accomplish for them and for the mission.

With your inventory and sequence in place, you can start sourcing stories that hit as many of your narrative beats as possible. You can refer back to Chapter 6 for guidelines here, but at a high-level, remember that your most compelling storyteller is always going to be a legacy donor, around the same age as your target audience, because they can hold the mirror up to your prospect. Of course, you don't ONLY have to use living bequesters (that being said, they will typically generate the best results). You want a good mix of voices – for example, a Board Member who left a gift, a lifelong volunteer, an alumnus, a beneficiary, the Executive Director, your founders. It's ideal if they've left a gift, but in some cases (like that student story above), it's just not realistic.

As you're choosing storytellers, make sure that their stories are powerful and align naturally with the storytelling inventory you've laid out. The best legacy stories are about personal connections to the cause. It's not enough for a storyteller to have left a gift in their will. They need to have done so for a deeply personal, passionate reason. Maybe arthritis runs in their family, so they're committed to finding a cure. Or perhaps they've sponsored 10 children over the years, and they want to continue supporting children after they're gone. The best legacy stories will be the ones that take place over a lifetime. And, taking the time to do your research upfront will make your life much easier down the line, when it comes time to actually write your letter.

Developing Mail Touchpoints for Legacy Prospects

Direct mail also has another huge bonus, in that it can be made to feel very personal indeed. A well-crafted legacy letter, written with the autobiographical brain in mind, can truly feel like it's been written from the desk of the signatory to a single recipient.

These letters will cultivate and persuade best if they're very personal (as opposed to institutional) and authentic (as opposed to corporate) in their sound and feel. Whenever you write legacy copy for any medium, just think of sitting with your elderly aunt at the kitchen table.

But no matter how powerful the story, how perfect the storyteller, or how well-written the story, none of it matters if the letter doesn't get opened. So, your legacy letters shouldn't just feel very different from your regular mail – they should look super different, too.

Think about what the letters that get sent in your regular direct mail program look like. What size envelopes do you use? Do you have a standard stock? How often are you using live stamps or hand addressing? Are they very colourful and visual? Try to identify what makes your mail look and feel like your mail – and then, in your legacy mailings, do something entirely different.

Are your regular mailings heavily-branded? We bet they are! Strip it back. Do you tend to use lots of imagery on your envelopes? Consider eliminating images and teasers altogether.

Remember, these packages need to feel authentic, like a one-to-one communication. So as you're assembling the package, ask yourself: Does it make sense for this storyteller to be sending a package that looks like this to the donor? And if you're not too sure, see what you can tweak to make your legacy mailings feel totally genuine – and totally different from anything else you send.

If it's done right, you might even find donors writing letters of their own back to the signatory, not realizing that the letter is a marketing piece!

PHONE

Even if you send the greatest legacy direct mail of all time, the reality is that most donors still won't share their intentions with you. Remember, for Civics, this is an intensely personal decision. For Boomers, it's much more about them than it is you.

Over the course of a legacy cycle, you can expect a 1-2% positive response rate (higher if it's your first kick at the can, lower if you're well on your way), and that range includes new expectancies, prospects, and suspects. You should expect a negative response rate, which includes your *"No, please don't send me any more mail,"* and *"I've done this but this gift isn't for you,"* in the 4-6% range.

That's where the phone comes in. As part of your cultivation cycle, find the perfect opportunity to pick up the phone and ask, respectfully, what their thoughts are about charitable bequests as a giving vehicle and/or if they're interested in making a gift in their will to you.

Two Types of Calling: Survey or Planned Giving Inquiry

There are two main types of calling campaigns you can undertake: a survey or a planned gift inquiry.

A traditional planned gift inquiry script is what most telemarketing suppliers will write for you and it's very direct. It is designed to specifically hone in on the donor's intentions, and will directly ask if the donor has, is planning to, or will consider leaving a gift in their will to your cause.

This should *never* be the first cultivation touchpoint. You need to prime donors with a steady series of raindrops on the roof before attempting this type of calling.

We find that donors can struggle with how forward this calling can be. Many donors consider speaking about their wills and their intentions to be a highly personal conversation — one that they likely haven't had with their own children or another human being other than their lawyer. It's private. It's not something you talk about. And it's most certainly something you don't talk about with a charity.

You want to be careful in employing this type of conversation that your callers are tactful and know when a donor is signaling to back off.

That being said, if you're early on in your legacy program (which we'd say would be in years one to five and executing your first to third calling campaign), this will be a highly effective tactic. Here, you will find out about the intentions of donors who are already familiar with this giving vehicle, love your charity, and need some (but not immense) persuasion to include you the next time they update their will. We find this calling skims the cream, so to speak, on your file, as the number of expectancies will likely outnumber the quantity of new leads generated. This can be really beneficial in demonstrating results and legacy potential that will help you secure future investment in your planned giving program.

Now, a survey is a very different type of calling. A survey allows you to plant mission-based questions, values-based questions, and gift vehicle questions under the guise of data-gathering. It may seem a bit sneaky, but the survey is designed to more informative for the donor than to actually solicit their opinions. It's best used with suspects and prospects who are close to your cause but haven't yet been persuaded that a gift in their will is the right mechanism for giving to you.

For example, we might ask a donor:

"More than 1.5 million Canadians have left a gift in their will and another 1 million Canadians are considering giving this way. Clearly making a gift in your will is a very popular way to give. Are you familiar with the concept of leaving gifts in wills?"

With a survey, we're planting seeds. We're designing questions to bring the donor closer to both the cause and to a specific way they can give. Depending on where you use this touchpoint in your cultivation cycle, you might never directly ask about their own personal intentions or plans.

This survey is best used with a larger group of donors that you're looking to qualify for future legacy communications and a particular donor journey. It will help you decide whether you can move an annual donor onto your legacy suspect or prospect conveyor belt, or from the suspect to prospect conveyor belt.

You can also design your survey for a smaller group of donors to find out their intentions after they've gone through a complete cultivation cycle. Here, the question becomes, *'Can you move a prospect to being a confirmed expectancy?'*. You may specifically want to craft questions that will have the donor engage in a conversation with you as you move closer and closer to asking if they've left a gift in the will for your charity.

An example of this type of question would be:

"You are an extremely loyal donor and have been contributing to this cause since 1999. Can you tell me a bit more about who taught you to be generous or where your generous spirit comes from?"

This is the perfect type of question to pull a donor into their autobiographical mindest. From there, it's a natural progression into a question about the legacy of generosity they may want to leave.

Whichever survey approach you use, or if you use both, we've found these to be effective with donors when designed thoughtfully and with purpose in moving them along in the cultivation process.

Final Thoughts on the Phone

Now, a word of warning: legacy telemarketing is a vastly different beast from regular telemarketing, just like legacy mail is totally different from your normal annual program mailings. Legacy calls tend to be much longer. Much like the letters, you'll find donors meander and chat much more than in a usual call. After all, you aren't talking about a gift – you're talking about their life! A good legacy caller will be able to go off-script and follow a donor's thought process, gently teasing out the key information you're looking for.

So it's paramount that you pick your vendor with care, if you're using one. Choose someone who's conducted successful legacy campaigns. Ask for legacy-specific references and case studies. Monitor closely and listen regularly to sample calls, and provide feedback as necessary (go with your gut, and prioritize the autobiographical brain!). Remember, to your donor, this is a conversation with *you*, not a telemarketing supplier, and it can be a sensitive topic – so a tactful, talented caller is key.

Because legacy giving is a highly personal subject, don't be surprised if a quarter to a half of the people you call aren't interested in talking with you about it. The important thing here is not to be pushy. After all, you're not selling magazine subscriptions!

Having said this, when done right, the phone is a powerful tool to swing open the door that your mailing will have just cracked open. We find that combining calling and the mail is the most effective way to add new prospects and suspects to your legacy pipeline, and you'll uncover a few new expectancies, too.

WEBSITE

As you're dripping letters, emails, and phone calls into your donor's world, there's a good chance that somewhere along the way, they'll consult your website. When they do, they'll be looking for one of two things – which means your web content needs to serve these purposes.

But let's not get ahead of ourselves. Before we create direct mail packages or phone campaigns, we first need to understand what makes a digital legacy audience so unique.

Who Uses Your Legacy Web Pages?

Legacy web content can be some of the trickiest to write. While your phone campaign or letter are designed to mimic a one-to-one conversation with your legacy prospect, your web content needs to be able to speak to two very distinct groups, who have two completely different sets of needs.

The first group of users is the most obvious: legacy prospects. Now, we know this can feel a little counter-intuitive. After all, your 79-year-old Auntie Edna struggles to work the remote for her TV, let alone do any significant Googling about leaving a gift in her will. But remember, you're now marketing legacy gifts as much to Boomers as you are to Civics. And Boomers are digitally-savvy!

What does this mean for you? It means that digital touchpoints are becoming a very key touchpoint in your legacy factory. Your online presence will become even more critical as Gen X and Millennials take their places in your legacy factory with intention in the next 20 to 30 years, but those who have already contemplated their own mortality are on a different timeline. So, start now!

These folks are seeking persuasive content more than instructional. They're following up on a legacy letter you sent. They're watching a video they saw you post on Facebook (and yes, your legacy prospect is on Facebook!). They read an article in your newsletter and want to learn more. They've read about your charity in the local community newspaper. Whatever drove them to your website, they have this in common: They have a gift in their will on the brain – and they're wondering if your organization is the right place to make a big impact.

Now, here's the kicker: Your prospect audience is your primary audience in every single legacy touchpoint – except your website. There is actually a second group of users who are larger and likelier to access your legacy web content: allied professionals.

That's right. Lawyers, accountants, and financial planners are truly the bread and butter of legacy web content. And most of them are looking for two key pieces of information: your legal name and your charitable registration number. You'd be surprised how hard it is to find these two pieces of key information – the legal details they need to put a gift to your organization in a client's will – on many charity websites (and no, that tiny text in your footer doesn't count as easy-to-find). For these folks, persuasive information simply doesn't matter. They need transactional info, and they need it fast.

Don't underestimate the need for this information and the need for lawyers to get it right. Imagine you have two charities with very similar names – Breast Cancer Care and Breast Cancer Campaign. It could be very easy for a donor to get the name wrong in their will and their gift could end up going to the wrong charity. It's happened. We have a story that goes around in our office of a long-time donor to a particular charity who let the charity know there was a gift in the will, and after she died it turned out she'd put the incorrect charity name and the funds went to an entirely different cause.

(As an aside, you'll also find the family of a donor who has passed away may be looking for this information, as well as a person to contact and your mailing address).

So, that's the challenge you face in crafting legacy web content. Two audiences. Two sets of completely different needs – one focused on the 'why,' the other focused on the 'how'. Your website needs to do both, and do both well. It needs to connect your donor with your mission, and connect your professionals with your charity in the most administrative sense of the word.

How do you do it? Read on.

Structuring Legacy Web Content

Before you write a single word of copy, ask yourself: how will anyone find this content?

Where you place this on your site matters. How you write it matters. Because if your legacy web content is too hard to find, you're missing out on key opportunities for prospects to tell you they're interested, and for professionals to make sure you get your money!

Try not to bury your legacy content deep in your website (but definitely host it on your site – microsites are decidedly of the 2000s). Your aim should be to make it so a person could find that content in no more than three clicks. Not only that, you want to ensure that you create all your legacy content (and it's headers and menu labels) with search optimization in mind.

Use best practice web writing – short sentences, plain language, and search-term optimized. This is a great time to dip into your Google Analytics and see what search terms actually bring people to your legacy pages, if you already have them. If not, think about how you'd search for it yourself.

The rule of thumb? Ditch industry phrasing, like 'planned giving', 'estate planning', and even 'legacy giving.' These mean nothing to donors. Just focus on 'gifts in wills', where 90-95% of your gifts will actually come from and what donors are most likely to be looking for, starting with your primary navigation.

In order to meet all the needs of both your audiences, you'll likely be looking at a few pages of content, so put some thought into how you want to connect those pages together. Will you have a primary legacy hub, with the other pages linked from there? Will each audience have their own page, or will you address both sets of needs on every page?

We like to lay out the architecture for legacy sections first, before we ever start writing, much like laying out the architecture for a whole website. It's a helpful way to identify the parameters of your current site, and then figure out how to best work within those limits to create content for both your legacy audiences.

Legal Information

We already talked about making sure your legal name and registration number are super-easy to find. Dropping the ball here is like a server who provides exceptional service all through the meal, then takes forever with the bill – it can ruin your whole experience.

So it's worth your while to eliminate that barrier as best you can. Put your legal name, charitable registration number, and address in a super-visible pull-out box in the legacy section on your website. Follow that up with your contact information, in case a prospect or planner has specific questions they need your input on. And for bonus points, create a downloadable one-pager that includes all of this information, that a prospect can print and hand right over to their lawyer.

Lead Generation

In addition to persuading prospects and giving professionals key information, your website has a third benefit: lead generation. You can use your site to gather the email addresses of folks who have raised their hand. By going to your site, they've indicated at least some interest in legacy giving (so, they're either suspects or prospects for your factory conveyor belts!)

We love to see organizations gathering email leads from their websites, because it enables you to bring email into your legacy factory. But first, you have to actually *get* the email address. And digital marketers will tell you that's getting harder and harder to do.

The most common lead generation tool when it comes to legacy is a form. We often use a version of your legacy reply coupon, adapted for a virtual space. This is a short form that asks donors to share their first name, email address, and their thoughts about making a gift in a will. Depending on their answer, they might get dropped into a variety of digital donor journeys (we'll talk about that more in a bit).

You can also invite donors to share an email address so they can start a conversation with you, or sign up for legacy emails from you. We typically avoid the most common lead generation tactics of offering content, like an e-book or one-pager, to avoid placing any barriers for those folks who are close to making the gift.

Regardless, we encourage you not to put the cart before the horse when it comes to lead generation. Make sure that you lay the foundation in your email program first, before you ever start acquiring digital leads, so that those folks can immediately begin to receive touchpoints when their interest and relevance is at an all-time high.

EMAIL

In this digital day and age, email has become one of the most versatile legacy touchpoints in your arsenal. It gives you options that mail and the phone simply can't: collecting real-time feedback through polls, directing folks to your website with trackable links, and best of all, embedding video that brings legacy giving to life. Plus, there is a level of automation that makes email especially convenient to execute, once it's up and running.

There are two main conveyor belts in your factory that benefit the most from email: your prospect belt and your pipeline belt. Let's dive into how you can use each one.

Persuasive Email

Email plays well with the prospect belt as a way to add email touchpoints to the persuasive phase of your legacy cultivation cycle. Email becomes yet another set of raindrops, tapping on the roof of the donor brain.

For prospects for whom you have both an email and a mailing address, you'll want to integrate both tactics together, from both a timing and a content perspective. Make sure that each touchpoint has breathing room around it (so, avoid a letter in the mailbox on the same day as there's an email in the inbox). And be sure that the content feels consistent between both channels, particularly when it comes to stories.

The real power is when you can use email to elevate your mailings or other touchpoints. When you can create that level of cohesion across multiple channels, the prospect conveyor belt will really start to hum. For example, you might send a letter from a living donor – and a couple weeks later, an email follows with a video from the signatory, so donors can feel even closer to that storyteller.

You might also end up with prospects for whom their legacy marketing journey is digital only, at least until you're able to acquire a mailing address or phone number for them. Naturally, you'll want their touchpoints to be more robust, dripping at a higher frequency to compensate for the other missing channels.

In this case, when you sequence your digital touches in advance, you want to be very intentional about how each email builds on the other. You need to account for the ease with which emails are ignored (much more easily than a legacy letter), so you can't simply take your direct mail plan and convert it to a series of emails. Think about how the full journey is experienced, but more importantly, think about the experience if the donor only opens half the emails, or never actually clicks, and so on.

Identification Email

Email is a surprisingly powerful tool for identifying new prospects. Now, we know it might sound a bit weird. If you already have an email, haven't you already identified the prospect? The reality is, not quite.

If you're using a form on your website to gather leads (and we hope you are, or will be!), email is a great tool to qualify those leads. After all, how are you to know where in the factory a new email address needs to go? Are they a suspect? A prospect? Imagine giving suspect touchpoints to a confirmed expectancy! Yikes. Hence, the need for qualification.

We like to use a survey sent via email for this. In fact, it's usually the very first email folks receive after the consent confirmation email. With a few carefully selected and sequenced questions, you can tease out exactly how your brand-new subscriber feels about gifts in wills — which tells you as a marketer what they need to hear from you to move forward in their journey. Once you know that, you can drop them into the digital donor journey that makes the most sense for them.

And once you have that survey email, and its subsequent automations, built and firing, we suggest you turn it to your other audiences! You likely have qualified leads sitting in your email list that you don't even know about. Your survey email is like a metal detector, seeking out those nuggets of legacy gold hiding right under your nose.

Now, we don't necessarily want you to take a shotgun approach here and send this legacy survey to every email in your database. Depending on how much info you have about your subscribers, we encourage you to segment for better tracking and trend analysis. But there's no harm in working your way through a large portion of your email list here, because the survey will inevitably have an opt-out that will immediately cull out anyone who isn't a good prospect. No harm, no foul.

Journey Mapping

So, you've gathered your emails and qualified them with a survey. Here's where email's biggest boon comes into play. It's time to automate!

Your goal here is to create an email donor journey that is appropriate for each stage of the donor journey. There are different ways to do this: you might start with a journey for each of your conveyor belts (so, newbies, suspects, and prospects). If your survey included a version of your reply coupon, you might add more nuance by crafting an automation for each possible response. And if you're really excelling, and you have different segmented donor groups, you might want to design journeys that correspond to each group.

Regardless of how many automations you build and how nuanced the segmentation is for each one, they'll be similar at a high-level. This particular email series will be much longer than a regular welcome or marketing automation – several months, maybe even a year. There will be much more space between each email than a typical automation, too, given the longer timeline. These emails should maintain that super-personal feel of all your other touchpoints (just because you're automating, doesn't mean it's time to become an organizational automaton!)

As always, ensure that every email has a goal: to drive a prospect to your website and generate traffic, to take a survey or answer a poll question, or to watch a video, for example. Legacy email, like all marketing emails, should have a concrete action for the donor to take.

But most importantly, aim to integrate your automations together. Just like your conveyor belts can shift a suspect to the prospect belt, your automations should be able to as well if you're using a sophisticated enough email tool. You can use if/then logic here to dictate how a person should move between automations, based on how they're interacting (or not) with your emails.

For example, say you've qualified a lead as a warm prospect through your survey mechanism. But three emails into the stream, they haven't clicked a single thing. You can't know for sure, but based on their behaviour, it seems like this messaging isn't resonating. So, perhaps you automatically shift them into the suspect stream, where the messaging is more impact-focused and drips at a slower rate.

If they click on the next email, you know you're on the money. But if another 2 or 3 touchpoints go by with no response, perhaps this lead simply isn't as qualified as you thought – perhaps you automatically remove them from the automation.

Now, this kind of donor journey mapping is complex and there isn't a single right way to do it. There will be trial and error in terms of content, timing, qualifying, segmentation – pretty much every variable. Every list is unique, so what works for one probably won't for another. Take your time, be patient, and benchmark against yourself. We promise it's worth the work!

OTHER USEFUL TOOLS

At the core, you want to be using a combination of direct mail, phone, and email in your legacy marketing. But you can elevate your legacy marketing in a variety of ways, including:

- A legacy booklet that combines lots of why and a bit of how (about 80% to 20%, respectively), which you can send to prospects who request more information.

- Piggybacking legacy content into existing touchpoint, like a legacy buckslip in your thank-you letters, or a living donor testimonial in your newsletters.

- An emotional, autobiographical video that shares the story of a living donor, while bringing the need to life and illustrating the all-important future need.

PUTTING IT ALL TOGETHER

At its core, what we're talking about here is a drip marketing program. Do you remember our metaphor about raindrops on the roof?

In Chapter 3, we talked about the importance of sending a steady drumbeat of legacy giving messages to your target audience – over and over and over – over the course of five to ten years. Why? Because your prospect has to be past the death avoidance stage to even begin to be receptive to considering a gift that is tied to their death. They need to be ready to engage in symbolic immortality. You also need your charity and how it aligns with their autobiography to be top of mind when the day does come to update their will. How can a single campaign actually address these key elements of legacy persuasion? Frankly, it can't.

In other words, a single mail or phone campaign approach is a five-minute thunderstorm when you need it to rain all day long.

Your tactical plan needs to be a long, slow burn, so that when you donor is updating their will — accounting for the birth of a grandchild perhaps, or moving into an assisted living facility after the death of their spouse — you'll be top of mind.

That means you want to pop up with legacy touchpoints regularly. Our typical rule of thumb is about every three months for your highest-quality prospects, and every six for other, cooler suspects. So look at the stories and storytellers you have available, and the tactics you want to use, and design a cycle that fits your resources *and* meets your prospects' needs.

We've walked you through the four primary tactics we use to marketing legacy giving: mail, phone, email, and website. We've talked about how mail integrates with phone, or how email integrates with mail. But we haven't really talked about how you take all four tactics and bring them together for a seamless cultivation cycle. In fact, we haven't even really told you how to prioritize your tactics.

We know it's probably a burning question you have. But there's a reason we haven't answered it. We've tried really hard as we've written this book to avoid that standard consultant answer, but in this case it's really true: It depends.

The tactics you pick – and more than that, the way you integrate them – completely depends on the maturity of your legacy program, the dollars you're able to invest and the staff resources you have to support it. The way we'd approach it if you're brand new to legacy marketing is vastly different than if you've been casually marketing for seven years, or aggressively marketing for the past two. If you have one part-time staff member, then what you can do is vastly different than if you have a team of four. That context is absolutely vital to deciding how you want to put your tactics together.

When we work with charity clients, whether they're large or small, we like to start building the foundations of a sustainable legacy marketing program that, once built, will last for years. Because, at the end of the day, the money goes to the charity that has the discipline and the patience to stick with a consistent strategy over many years.

Legacy fundraising is a marathon – not a sprint!

So, take stock of where you are now. And, consider what it is your factory needs from you. Which belt needs the most attention? Maybe you have a huge jam of prospects who simply aren't getting to yes. Or maybe your pipeline belt is pretty slim, so you barely have enough donors to keep the rest of the factory ticking. Let the gaps in your pipeline guide you in selecting and integrating the tools you need most.

The important thing is that you use a mix of all the tools above to help forge the connection between your organization and a gift in the will, in the mind of your donor. Let each tactic augment the other, and don't be afraid to implement several simultaneously, rather than sequentially.

SEGMENTING YOUR LEGACY RESPONDERS

As you start receiving responses to your legacy identification questions, you're going to find that you now have four groups of people – and that each of these groups merits a different kind of attention.

Expectancies

These are the people who have told you in no uncertain terms that they have already included you as a beneficiary in their will. These people no longer need to be persuaded to make a bequest (which has been the main thrust of your messaging so far). Do keep in mind though, that these people may well increase the size of their bequests in the years to come!

If we go back to our legacy factory, once the donor has put up their hand and said, *"Yes! I've left you a gift in my will,"* these folks hop off the prospect conveyor belt and hop onto the expectancy one. This belt is a never-ending loop where donors are served gratitude and impact messaging.

What they now need is to continually hear about how you are advancing your mission. Your principal job is simply to reinforce the reasons why they put you in their will in the first place – the same way that car advertisements aren't designed to convince you to buy a car, but instead to reassure recent purchasers that they made the right call. Your mission aligns with their concern about the cause. You achieve positive results with donated dollars. You have plans to move the mission further ahead with your next initiatives.

It's worth noting that many planned giving fundraisers we talk with express concern that if they don't do enough stewardship, the donor might remove the charity from their will. Generally speaking, this is not the case for donors.

When donors remove charities from their wills (which in our experience is a rare event), it's because the charity itself has messed up in a big way. The donor will only remove the charity from the will if their trust is broken, because of a scandal or some other egregious behaviour – not because they didn't get enough thank you messages from the fundraising department.

IF ONLY WE HAD A CRYSTAL BALL...

This book is mostly about Boomers and Civics. They are where the legacy money is right now. And frankly, they're where it's going to continue to be for the next 20 years. But we already have clients who are taking the extra-long view, marketing gifts in wills to Gen X and even Millennials. The reality is, we simply don't know if these groups will be more likely to take a gift out of their will. We're looking at a much longer time of realization – upwards of 40 to 70 years – with at least three revisions to their will. In all that time, with all those updates, will these younger prospects start to remove gifts where their parents never did? Only time will tell.

What planned giving fundraisers never seem to think about is the possibility that the bequester might *increase* the size of the gift in her will at some point down the road – or the common trend that donors tend to increase their annual giving once they're made a gift in their will. In our opinion, *this* is a great reason to give great stewardship. In fact, if you could find a donor who has increased the amount of their charitable bequest, their testimonial would be a great one to throw into your mix!

Your expectancies are also worth getting to know on a more personal level because it is through telling their stories that will be able to keep your factory moving along. The living donor is the most effective story you have in your database to aid you in cultivating new legacy prospects and suspects – because in telling their story you allow the donor to hold that autobiographical mirror up to themselves.

So, your objective with expectancies is to keep the bequest where it is, and to grow it over time.

Prospects

These are the people who haven't made a gift in their will, but have told you that they're actively thinking about it. It's a no-brainer that this is your key audience for further persuasive communications – and this is the group that should receive the most generous share of your budget (at least on a per capita basis).

When we wrote *Iceberg Philanthropy* back in 2007, our radical idea was that charities could use direct marketing tactics (mass communications) to deliver a major gift strategy (moves management from cultivation to solicitation). This prospect audience is the perfect example of how you can employ this hybrid idea of direct response moves management.

We would argue that once you have found this audience – even if it's small at first – you should send them persuasive, legacy-specific messages at least four times a year. These messages can be personal (phone call or visit), print (letters work best), digital (video, stewardship reports or newsletters) or event-based (an invitation to a program briefing/update by your senior program staff).

Which brings us back to patience. We would try to identify a gift decision with this group at least once every two years, and we would keep actively marketing to these prospects for 10 or 20 years if necessary!

With your prospect group, always keep in mind that your objective is to persuade them to take that next step – to make the commitment and make the gift.

Suspects

This is the group that hasn't left a gift in their wills – nor have they indicated that they're actively considering making a bequest. Rather, this group has told you that *"I'm not thinking about a bequest now, but I might in the future."* Think of this group as the pot of stew on your stove top – it's not dinner time yet, but you want to keep it warm on the back burner. It's folks who perhaps are employing the 'distract' or 'delay' mode of death avoidance, because death is such a long way off.

In our view, these folks can get pretty much the same persuasive messages and materials as the prospect group – they just don't need too much of it. Plus, you don't want to invest as much money on people who are less likely to make gifts. So, if you're communicating with your prospects four times a year, you might want to communicate with your suspects twice a year. And while you should connect with your prospect group about every two years about their intentions, you might want to go back and identify where these folks are at in their decision making process every four years.

With your suspect group, your objective is to move them up one rung on the ladder. You're hoping that they'll tell you next time that they're thinking about making a bequest, which will move them up a level to prospect status.

Not Interested

Whenever you send out an identification form asking people to indicate their bequest inclinations, there will be a group of folks who tell you that they're simply not interested in this type of giving. In our experience, this group will often be the most numerous of any of the responses you receive.

Please don't be disheartened by this!

Keep in mind that only about 5-10% of your donors are going to make bequests – which means that 90-95% won't. Unlike other types of direct response marketing, legacy response rates are very low (often between 1% and 4% over a multi-year period), *but* the gift sizes are incredible. It's the size of the legacy gift (which averages about $35,000 in Canada) that makes this type of fundraising so lucrative.

Sometimes, fundraisers have the instinct to try to convince this 'no thanks' group to reconsider. We don't think this is a good use of your time, money and effort. What we'd rather see you do is to examine each of these people individually and ask yourself if there is any evidence available that suggests that this person might be a good candidate for monthly giving, mid-level giving, or a major gift.

RUBBER ON THE ROAD

If you can take some of the steps we've outlined in this chapter, you'll have some real traction established and you'll be moving forward with purpose and confidence. Just don't forget to stick to your strategy with discipline and patience. Your course is now set. The key moving forward is to stay consistent and keep those legacy raindrops falling!

CHAPTER 8:
STEWARDSHIP AND RECOGNITION OF EXPECTANCIES

In the last chapter, we talked about your legacy factory in two parts. In the first part of the factory, you're managing many pipelines that are all designed to persuade a prospect to leave a gift in their will and tell you about it.

In the second part of the factory, there's only one belt and it's on a permanent loop. When you've met that first goal – when your donor puts up their hand to say 'yes,' writes you into their will and confirms it with you – they move into the second part of the legacy factory.

That's where this chapter will focus: on the ongoing, lifelong process of stewarding your legacy donor (at least, your ability to steward the one donor of every eight who will actually tell you about their gift).

THE DIFFERENCE BETWEEN CULTIVATION AND STEWARDSHIP CONTENT

We've already talked a lot about what to do when you're cultivating and persuading legacy prospects. You have a certain message focus (remember the Good Works 40:30:20:10 Golden Rule?). Your job with prospects is to tell stories of people demonstrating their commitment to your cause and mission by making bequests. You're speaking to the autobiographical brain, and trying to align a bequest with the narrative that your prospect is creating about herself. You're planting seeds and being very patient as they germinate and grow inside the prospect's heart and mind.

When it comes to stewarding of those who have already made their bequests, your job is somewhat different. A donor who has included you in their will is using your organization's work to achieve symbolic immortality – and you now need to reassure them that through this gift, they will never be forgotten. You need to let them know that you'll be there to remember their lives, their work, their goodness, and their love.

It sounds like a tall order. But thankfully, donors have already told us loud and clear what they need from you!

As we talked about in the last chapter, expectancies should keep on getting direct mail asks – and they're likely to increase their annual giving to you once they've made a gift in their will. And direct mail donors have told us over and over again in focus groups that, more than anything, they want to be assured and reassured that their dollars achieve their intended purpose and make the world a better place.

So first and foremost, you want to keep demonstrating, as clearly and powerfully as you can, that donated dollars are getting results and forwarding your mission. Communicating impact with this group on an ongoing basis shows them you're legitimate, trustworthy, and a responsible steward of their money. It reassures them that they made the right decision by making your organization a part of their legacy!

Second, expectancies should hear stories about legacy gifts that you've received, how they've been invested, and how they've achieved results. This helps strengthen the connection between impact and legacy gifts, and helps them to envision the kind of impact they'll be able to have on the world even after they die.

Now, if you're a small to medium-sized shop, you can certainly use one communications vehicle – like a legacy newsletter, for example – to speak to both audiences. You can persuade prospects and steward donors with a thoughtful assortment of testimonials, profiles, stories, and information. Just keep both these groups in mind as you lay out your newsletter, and make sure that there's content for both.

LAYING OUT THE STEWARDSHIP PLAN

In an ideal world, you would have your stewardship approaches and plan all worked out *before* you start soliciting bequests. When that expectancy comes in, you want that stewardship conveyor belt already up-and-running, not stuck and stagnant!

But, we also know that that might be a tall order. You might not be able to take a long enough view to lay out all those touchpoints. It might be more realistic for your team to work them out one at a time. If that's the case for you, we'd suggest you identify at least that first touch. That will buy you some time to identify where the next stewardship piece should fall.

Now, these stewardship contacts can be many and varied. You could call to say thanks. You could extend an invitation to an event. You could send a newsletter, or a handwritten note, or an email. One of our clients sends a personally signed copy of a book penned by the Chair of their legacy giving society. The list is pretty much endless. Ask yourself: what is meaningful to your supporters and can further deepen their connection to your charity?

We've often found it helpful to include stewardship in the guiding principles document we talked about in Chapter 4. After all, if stewarding is half of your factory, it should certainly be included in the core manifesto of your legacy marketing program! What if you adopted a principle that 'each known bequester will receive at least three stewardship contacts per year until the gift is received?' This can make buy-in much easier down the line when you're trying to feature a legacy testimonial in a newsletter. Plus, it helps you hold yourself accountable to the commitment you've made to your legacy donors!

LET THE DONOR BE YOUR GUIDE

For the most part, your legacy donors are going to resemble Jacqueline and Kevin. Even though they've just chosen you to be the recipient of (by far) the largest gift they'll ever give, there's a good chance that they've never made a charitable gift of more than $100 during their lifetime. So, many of your new expectancies are not used to any sort of special attention other than the form letter thank you they get with their tax receipts. That's not what they've come to expect from you.

Then, there are demographics to consider. For your Civic donors, keep in mind the modesty and humility that comes with Jacqueline's Judeo-Christian ethic. Jacqueline was raised to do her good works quietly and modestly. She was taught not to be boastful or to bring unnecessary attention to herself. In fact, many religious traditions place a higher spiritual value on those gifts and good deeds that remain anonymous. To many older people, the highest order of generosity goes unnoticed and unrewarded.

These donors don't want grand gestures They don't think of themselves as famous philanthropists, and they don't want to be treated that way. They want authenticity, simplicity, and impact.

For your Boomer donors like Kevin, however, their desire to give is more motivated by the individual need to give. They like to be made to feel special and unique (even if they'd never admit it). Don't make too much of a fuss or give too much attention, but give just enough to indicate that you know who they are and why they are important to your cause.

Where a Civic donor might be mortified that you mention their bequest at a Board meeting while they're still alive, a Boomer would be a little tickled pink.

For donors like Kevin, you may want to email them a funny meme you've seen on the internet that speaks to a past conversation you've had, or mail them a copy of an article highlighting research they support at your institution with a handwritten covering note. Even better, ask them for their thoughts on a new stewardship touchpoint you're considering. Would they find getting a signed copy of an art print meaningful? They particularly love ways to get involved.

So what does all of this mean for you as you're stewarding a legacy donor? Well, Jacqueline and Kevin should be made to feel special – after all, they've done a very special and noble thing. But your job is to make them feel special on their terms. It's not to make yourself feel that you've made them special — and that's a harder line than it seems!

Many of the fundraisers we know seem to want to shower their legacy donors with all sorts of recognition. And we understand it! It's natural to want to celebrate a legacy donor's incredible commitment — especially when you know, firsthand, just how much work went into moving them along in the factory.

Yet, the donors we've spoken with, and listened to in focus group, often aren't so keen on the idea. Why do we have this gap?

In fundraising, we have been raised on the idea of paying more attention to donors as their gifts get bigger. As gifts go from $50 to $100 to $500 to $5,000 to $50,000, we make more and more fuss over the people who give those gifts. There's a logic to this, and we understand it.

But we aren't talking major gifts here, at least in the traditional fundraising sense. So that logic just isn't appropriate when it comes to a gift in a will.

Instead, we encourage you to go back to Chapter 2: Identifying Your Legacy Donor and Chapter 5: The Giving Brain here as you create your stewardship plan. Think about their values. Think about how their gift fits into their life story. And create a stewardship plan that works for them, not for you. With that in mind, we'd like to take the opportunity to talk about some of the most common legacy stewardship tactics — and take a hard look at whether or not they really have the donor at heart.

Legacy Events

By the logic we've set out above, the average legacy donor is a pretty ordinary person, living a pretty straightforward life. They're not, for the most part, the cocktail reception and gala evening types at all. You need to be sensitive and thoughtful about what kinds of events and activities you invite them to participate in.

Having said that, these donors do love events! We often hear from legacy donors in interviews that events are a highlight of their year, and make them feel really good about their gift. It simply needs to be the right *kind* of event.

Our rule of thumb for donor stewardship when it comes to events is to keep things mission-focused rather than recognition-focused. Your Jacquelines and Kevins would rather come to an afternoon luncheon to hear a heart surgeon talk about the non-invasive procedures he's now able to perform thanks to donor dollars, than to come to a black-tie evening to celebrate your biggest campaign donors. They'd rather you send them a copy of a news release with a personal note, or ask them for their opinion on a new program or service. Events that bring them behind the curtain and confirm that they're helping to advance your mission are the name of the game here.

Now, this is a simplistic approach, we know – but we think it's a good place to start when you're asking yourself when and where you'd like to include your expectancies in existing donor stewardship plans.

Legacy Societies

Fundraisers ask us all the time whether or not it's essential that they set up a special legacy society to recognize bequest donors before they start their actual marketing efforts. Our answer is an emphatic NO!

Now, if you already have a legacy society, that's fine. But your most loyal donors make their bequests to you because of their commitment to your cause and their faith in your ability to advance your mission. They do *not* make bequests to get a gold pin or an invitation to a reception.

If your charity doesn't have a legacy society, we don't think you need one. There are a hundred other priorities that are more deserving of your time, effort, and money.

Donor Walls

When we do donor focus groups and talk about the idea of legacy giving, we're struck at how concerned donors are with confidentiality and privacy. We've already talked about the Judeo-Christian ethic of anonymity. But, there's another concern that donors have. Many of your legacy donors and prospects, particularly the Civics, are concerned that if their names are published as legacy donors, they'll be hounded by the other 90,000 charities in Canada to make bequests to them too.

And that's not the only place a donor wall can fall short. We've talked about how the key to legacy stewardship is to make the donor feel special, important, one-of-a-kind (especially your Boomers!). A legacy wall plops that donor's name – and their gift – into a long list of other donors and gifts. Maybe it even puts them into tiers of generosity. Is that truly the way to make a donor feel special – by lumping them in the gift of their life with everyone else's? We don't believe it is.

Our advice to charities that are just beginning to market legacy gifts is this: Rather than setting up a legacy society, focus on guaranteeing privacy and confidentiality to your bequest donors if they want it. We think that your marketing materials, be they print, broadcast or digital should reassure prospects that you will respect their desire to keep their bequests private.

WHY DONORS REVOKE GIFTS

Many of the fundraisers we talk to, especially those in smaller and mid-sized charities, are reluctant to get too assertive with their legacy marketing efforts. They worry that if they don't give their bequesters *lots* of attention and special treatment, those bequesters will revoke their gifts and go elsewhere.

We've never seen any evidence that this is the case.

As we've already said, your legacy donors want to continue to see evidence that you're advancing your mission and that you spend donated dollars wisely and effectively. They don't expect or need hand-written thank you notes or invitations to events.

Occasionally (and we think it's a rare occurrence) donors *do* revoke their charitable bequests. But, they don't do so because they find their stewardship lacking. Rather, bequesters revoke their gifts if their confidence and trust in the charity itself is shaken. If your charity's leadership is involved in a personal scandal or if your organization is near bankruptcy, your donors might get cold feet.

But they're not going to bail on you because they didn't get an invitation to the garden party in June. Remember the Golden Rule. Their gift is about their own life stories and about your cause and mission. Those things run a lot deeper than thank you notes and your charity's social event calendar.

THINK OFFENCE RATHER THAN DEFENCE

As we've already said, many (if not most) planned giving fundraisers see bequester stewardship as a defensive tactic. By this we mean that these fundraisers see stewardship as a means of hanging on to those legacy gifts that have already been made.

But as we talked about with your legacy factory, we look at stewardship in a more optimistic and assertive way. We don't see the revelation of a bequest commitment as the end of the road at all. It might, in fact, be just the beginning of a whole new relationship.

We have two other important ideas about why you should be strategic in your stewardship of legacy donors.

Inspiring Others with the Story

If you are going to build a truly first-class legacy program at your charity, you'll do it by creating a strong storytelling culture. Every bequest commitment you receive is a part of someone's life story. It's an important part of his or her autobiography. And, every one of these stories has the potential to inspire many other donors and supporters to make bequests themselves.

We encourage you to have a mindset that your stewardship program should foster intimacy, confidence, and trust in your legacy donors that they will become more willing to share their story with others. At first, most will be reluctant to have the spotlight put upon themselves. But, if you frame the conversation properly, you'll help them see how much sharing their story will help to inspire others and to advance your mission.

Today's expectancy is tomorrow's signatory.

Cultivating Bigger Annual Gifts and a Bigger Bequest Down the Road

Most planned giving fundraisers we talk to see stewardship from a problematic rather than an opportunistic mindset. As a legacy fundraiser, it's highly unlikely that your bequesters are going to bail on you once they've put you in the will. So, you don't need to worry about that much.

But, there's another opportunity that we rarely talk about! If you continue to build your bequester's confidence in you, they could very well *increase* the size of their gift in the years to come.

They will also likely *increase the size of their annual gifts to you.* We quickly talked about this in Chapter 7, and will go into more detail here.

In her 15-year study of donors at a large American charity, Susan DameGreen discovered that donors who were cultivated after the initial thank you for their charitable bequest gave 3 to 4 times as much. Our clients also report that planned gift donors tend to increase the size of their annual gifts after confirming their bequest. Now that's a great reason for great stewardship!

So when you're asking planned giving donors for an annual gift, don't forget to acknowledge their legacy gift. Be intentional and thoughtful about which asks they get from the annual program – perhaps they should no longer receive every mailing or email – and then customize these as much as possible to speak to the donor as a planned gift donor first. You need to both acknowledge the immense power of their future gift while asking them to give again to make a difference today.

Again, here's where demographics come into play again. As your Civic donors move into retirement homes or long-term care facilities, they may no longer have the cash flow to make annual gifts. In fact, they may ask that you no longer send them solicitations because they feel guilty when they can't give. This doesn't mean they don't want to hear from you, it just means you should only send stewardship mailings. A two-year lapse in annual giving is often a flag that your expectancy is approaching the end of their life.

As for your Boomer legacy donors, don't think twice about wooing and wowing and asking them to continue to make (and stretch) with their annual gifts.

DON'T FORGET – THEY'RE STILL ALIVE!

We want to close this chapter by encouraging you not to make the mistake of assuming that your bequest donors should now be put on your shelf until they, well, die and leave you the money.

Even if Jacqueline makes her bequest commitment to you at age 65 or 75, she still has lots of charge in her life's battery. She's probably only on her 2nd or 3rd will – meaning she has, on average, two more updates to go.

She has just made what we consider to be the ultimate statement of her commitment and trust in your organization and its mission. It's not time to back off now. Instead, she should absolutely be encouraged and invited to keep making annual gifts since many bequesters increase their annual giving.

You'll remember that this book is based on a donor-centred premise. Our marketing approach always starts and ends with the donor – their values and beliefs, their hopes and dreams, their memories and relationships, their faith and philosophy.

You should do everything you can once you've received a bequest intention notification to talk to your new legacy donor and find out everything you can about them. Picture yourself a tailor who's going to custom-make an outfit for Jacqueline. Your job now is to customize a relationship with – and an experience for – Jacqueline that will be meaningful, joyful, and fulfilling.

After all, you have been given the gift of helping to craft the epilogue to Jacqueline's wonderful autobiography. You are helping to shape the final chapter in the story of her life. This will be the most rewarding work you'll probably ever do as a fundraiser. You need to keep showing the impact of the dollar on the cause, and you also need to keep showing that you're a responsible, effective steward of that dollar.

We encourage you to appreciate and savour every moment of this beautiful task.

CHAPTER 9:
HOW TO MODEL YOUR LEGACY ROI

As you can certainly see by now, we really do come at legacy fundraising from the donor's perspective. We work feverishly to understand the donor's heart and mind. We take a craftsman's pride at how we fashion and polish messages that will resonate just-so with your legacy prospects. To us, legacy gift communications is an art just as beautiful and demanding as songwriting or creating poetry.

This chapter is about the business side of legacy gift marketing. It's about the investment you need to make, the return that investment will generate and the time frame over which you will recoup your ROI.

We'll warn you now that we're going to be just a little geeky with our math – but we promise that we're going to make it as simple and digestible as we possibly can.

WHY THIS CHAPTER MATTERS

If you're like 99% of the legacy fundraisers we know, you have to justify your existence. You need to go through a budget cycle in which there are lots of competing demands for scarce dollars. When you go to your Executive Director or VP of Finance or Board chair to ask for a legacy budget, they're going to ask *'How much will this raise?'* followed by *'When will we see the money?'*

At first blush, it's a tough pitch to make. After all, up to 90% of your bequesters won't tell you about their gifts — and those that do include you in their wills aren't planning on dying tomorrow.

You won't impress your Board by saying, *"Well, I really have no idea how much this will make because they won't tell us. But, we should have most of the money in the next 25 years or so!"* That just won't fly.

So, let's find another way to come at this, shall we?

We have spent many years working with our clients to estimate, predict, and model how their legacy revenues will take shape once they start planning and executing a proactive and consistent legacy marketing strategy. We'd like to share our methodology with you now, so that you can create your own ROI model — and use it to persuade your organization's leadership that a consistent legacy investment makes very good sense!

If you follow this 10-step approach, you'll be well on your way to having your very own ROI model built. And to make your life even easier, we've modelled an example for you, using Awesome Birding Canada (ABC), to show you what this looks like in action.

1. Do a Constituent Census

The first thing you want to do is to count heads and determine how many supporters you have in your database. Now, we almost always start with annual donors (who give via mail, phone, and digital channels). We like to include one-time (or single-gift) donors as well as monthly donors.

With that as your base, you can then add segments of people where it makes sense for your organization. Volunteers are certainly a good bet in our opinion, as are members (if you have them). You may or may not want to include event donors (do they support your organization or just like to play golf or dress up for galas?) or tribute/memoriam donors (who usually give once and never again to honour a loved one).

Once you're done, you'll have a count – a number – of those constituents from whom you might receive a bequest. Your first step is done!

EXAMPLE: ABC determines that it has 24,000 donors and volunteers who are reasonable 'suspects' for legacy giving.

2. Estimate the Number of Will-makers

Now that you know how many 'legacy-eligible' supporters you have in your database, the next thing you need to do is to estimate how many of them actually have wills. We know from repeated polling of adult Canadians that the older you get, the more likely you are to have a will. For example, very few people in their 20s have wills, while about 90% of people aged 60+ have wills.

As a starting point, if direct mail donors are a significant part of your supporter constituency, it's a very good bet that most of them are over 50 years old. In this case, we would normally estimate that 80% of them have wills.

If 80% is your estimated percentage, then you multiply it by your number of constituents from step 1. Now you have the estimated number of supporters with wills.

EXAMPLE: Since ABC has a robust direct mail program, it can safely assume most of its donors are over the age of 50. To be conservative, it estimates that 75% of its supporters have wills. This leaves them with 18,000 ABC donors who also have made wills.

3. Derive the Number of Charitable Bequest Gift-makers

Now, we turn our attention to actual charitable bequests. The next question we need to ask is '*How many of my supporters with wills have made bequests to charities?*'

Based on our *2019 State of the Legacy Nation* research which we reviewed in Chapter 2, we know that 17% of Canadians with wills make bequests to charity. So, if you multiply your result from step 2 (the number of your supporters with wills) by 17%, you will determine the number of your supporters who have made bequests to charities.

EXAMPLE: Multiplying their 18,000 legacy-eligible supporters by 17% means that ABC has 3,060 supporters are charitable bequesters.

4. Estimate the Total Number of Charitable Bequests

Next, we want to figure out how many actual legacy gifts your charitable bequesters have made to different charities. While there are no quantifiable research results out there, we've done a lot of anecdotal research (which means we've talked to *many* planned giving fundraisers and allied professionals) and we believe that the average legacy donor leaves bequests to four charities.

So, if you choose to use our number, you multiply your number of charitable bequesters (from step 3) by 4. This is the total number of bequest gifts that your supporters have made.

EXAMPLE: ABC assumes that each of their 3,060 bequesters has made four gifts. Therefore, the total estimated number of charitable bequests made by ABC supporters is 12,240.

5. Convert Gifts to Revenue

Now, we want to convert the number of gifts into the dollar value those gifts represent. In order to do this, you'll need to multiply your number of bequest gifts (that you determined in step 4) by your average bequest gift amount.

If your charity receives lots of bequests, you've probably already calculated your average bequest gift amount. If you've done this, by all means you should use your own number. But, if you don't get that many bequests (yet!) or haven't done the analysis, you could use the sector-wide average of $35,000 as a starting point.

Multiply the number of bequest gifts (from step 4) by $35,000 (or your own average if you have one) to estimate the total amount of bequest revenue that your supporters will leave to charities when their time comes to depart this world.

EXAMPLE: When ABC multiplies the 12,240 bequests by $35,000, the total bequest revenue to all charities from ABC supporters is estimated at $428.4 million.

6. Target Your Share

So, you've estimated how much money your supporters have left to all the charities and causes that they support, the question becomes: *How much will they leave to you?*

The answer to this question is a largely subjective one, but we think that there's a range in which your charity probably falls. If your prospect supports 20 charities overall, the odds are that you'll receive a 5% share of their bequest money. We would see this as the base amount that you should seek.

If your brand is more powerful (like a community hospital for example) or established (like the Canadian Cancer Society, Red Cross or World Wildlife Fund), we think you could target 10% of that revenue. We can tell you that, with every single client we've worked with to date, we've set a revenue target somewhere between 5% and 10% of the total legacy dollars available.

EXAMPLE: ABC feels that it's entirely achievable to 'win' 5% of that legacy revenue their supporters are leaving to charities. So, their long-term revenue goal is $21.4 million ($428.4 million x 5%).

7. Amortize Annual Revenue

At this point, we've determined the overall revenue you're seeking to achieve. But, that revenue is going to come to you over an extended period of time. Your Executive Director or VP of Finance are going to ask you what that's going to mean on an annual basis.

Our answer to this is a very simple one. We encourage our clients to '*amortize*' their revenue over a generation – or a 20-year timeframe.

This step involves taking your overall revenue target (from step 6) and dividing it by 20 in order to get an annual revenue outcome.

EXAMPLE: Now that ABC has its overall legacy goal of $21.4 million, it amortizes that amount over 20 years to arrive at an estimated annual revenue target of $1.07 million.

8. Apply Cash Flow Timing

When we do this process with clients, we often get asked 'When will we start seeing this money?' Again, there are no definitive empirical research findings to base an answer on, but we can make an educated guess. We've talked with many, many planned giving fundraisers, and we've pored over actuarial probability of death tables (the kind that life insurance companies use).

If you have an established legacy program (let's say 10+ years), then you'll likely be able to calculate an average time between when your donor notifies you that you're included in their will till the time that you are notified by an executor that the individual has died. We see a range of 2-8 years with our current clients. You can start your revenue modelling here.

Now, if you're new to legacy giving, we recommend that you take a different approach. Starting with our annual revenue target (from step 7) as a baseline, here's how we'd anticipate new legacy revenue coming in.

- Allow two years for your program to ramp up and your persuasive messages to sink in.

- Allow two more years for prospects to actually go to their lawyers and write your gift into their wills

- In the fifth year, you should start to see some revenue growth. We would expect you to see 25% of your annual revenue target in year five.

- In year six, we'd expect to see 50% of your annual revenue target.

- In year seven, we'd expect to see 75% of your annual revenue target.

- Finally, in year eight, you should hit 100% of your annual revenue target. This new revenue level should now maintain itself for a good 12-15 years. This is the time in which you will become a legend at your organization!

9. How Much Investment?

In spite of our best efforts, this is the second place in this book where we have to give you the standard consultant's answer of *'it depends'*. But when you ask us how much you'll have to spend on your program, it really does depend on a wide range of variables, such as the size of your constituency, the existing communications channels that you can leverage, the age of your supporters, and so on.

Having said that, we'll offer you a rough idea here of how you might frame some realistic expectations on your legacy expenditure budget:

- Go back to your 'constituent census' supporter population that you calculated in step 1. For ABC, that was 24,000.

- Take 25% of that number and multiply it by $12 per year for three years. In the case of ABC, 25% of their supporters adds up to 6,000 people. So 6,000 people x $12 x 3 years = an investment of $216,000 on the part of ABC.

- Take 75% of that number and multiply it by $2 per year for three years. Following this logic, ABC will target 18,000 supporters over 3 years with an investment of $108,000.

When you add your two results together, you'll have a ballpark figure as to how much you'll have to invest to 'move the needle' and actually persuade your supporters to make their bequests to you.

Using the expenditure formula laid out in step 9 of the previous sequence, ABC will invest $324,000 over three years to generate a return of $21.4 million. This investment represents a cost per dollar raised of less than 2 cents. (Now, to be fair, ABC will have to continue to invest in communications with legacy prospects and donors beyond three years – but even if we double the investment over time, the cost per dollar raised is still less than a nickel!)

10. Comparing ROI to the Gala and Golf Tournament

Every fundraising tactic your charity employs has an ROI. Most charities we know use the inverse measure of Cost Per Dollar Raised (often referred to in fundraiser jargon as CPD).

Many of the tactics we use in fundraising are not terribly efficient in terms of generating lots of net revenue. Direct response fundraising often has a CPD of 40 or 50 cents. Special events often have a CPD of 50 cents or more – as do charitable gaming and lotteries.

Other types of fundraising – like monthly giving, mid-level giving, and major gifts – are much more efficient. Sometimes they get to a point where their CPD is as low as 10 or 15 cents.

But in our experience, a properly planned and executed legacy program for all but the smallest charities can be achieved at a CPD of *three to five cents!* We have never – ever – found a more efficient and effective way to raise money than to plan and implement a multi-year legacy gift marketing strategy.

SUMMING UP

Before we conclude this chapter, we want to strongly encourage you to do two things:

First, spend enough time with this ten-step process to actually understand it. It really is simple and logical once you get it – and once you get it, you'll have it forever.

Then, once you understand the methodology, don't be afraid to adjust some of the numbers to suit your particular situation. For example, if you're an environmental advocacy organization, your donors might be younger – and there might be fewer of them who have wills. Or, if you're a community hospital foundation, you might want to estimate your average bequest gift amount at $80,000 instead of $35,000. (Hospitals, universities, and performing arts institutions usually have average bequest amounts of $80,000, $100,000 or even more – while social service agencies might average $17,000 or $22,000.)

The key of this chapter is that this methodology is the best available in the sector today to estimate your legacy revenue potential – and your ROI. We think it's your fiduciary duty to do this work well and to be transparent with it.

From a 'small-P' political point of view, this work is also very important to ensure that your internal leadership and stakeholders are fully supportive of your efforts to build a successful legacy gift marketing program.

CHAPTER 10:
MAKING LEGACY GIVING
AN OFFICE PRIORITY

There's a great irony to today's legacy fundraising landscape. It's your classic *"on the one hand, on the other hand…"* scenario.

On the one hand, there are tens of billions of dollars in play. There are about a million and a half legacy donors in Canada. There are opportunities galore – and! – the marketplace isn't yet crazy-crowded like just about every other type of fundraising available to you. That's the good news.

But, on the other hand, there are undoubtedly people (maybe lots of them) within your organization who just don't get it. Many, if not most, of our leaders are under incredible pressure to deliver dollars now – this month, this quarter, this year. Many of the charities we talk to are in a sort of dystopian mode of philanthropy – where the next transaction is paramount, and long-term relationships and horizontal ROI simply aren't the priority.

This chapter is about helping you to get smart — no, *wise* — decisions made within your organization. It's about the politics of building a legacy gift marketing program. It's about securing that all-important buy-in that will sustain you until your bequest revenue growth provides all the fuel you're going to need.

So here, in no particular order, are some of the tried-and-true ways we've found to help you get everyone at your non-profit on board with legacy.

SHOWING INCREDIBLE VALUE

You probably already know how it goes. You attend a great legacy session at a conference — or you read a great article (or book like this one!) and you get all cranked up about legacy gift marketing. You see the potential for your organization. In fact, you see it all so clearly now that it's pretty much a no-brainer that you should be doing much more than you are now.

So, you go to your boss and make your pitch. But rather than shared excitement, you get this blank gaze. *"You want us to spend HOW much? And when EXACTLY will we see these donations?"*

The trouble here is that your boss is so hunkered down on meeting this quarter's revenue target that she just can't see years down the road. The idea of truly stewarding and sustaining your organization's mission for the next generation evaporated somewhere after the financial markets melted down in 2008.

We recommend that, rather than pitching legacy revenues on their own, you present bequests within a portfolio format. After all, your boss probably has an RRSP – and knows something about balancing portfolios. Your argument here is that some of your fundraising tactics, like events, raise quick money, but the return on investment is ridiculously low. Marketing bequests, on the other hand, offers an incredible return on investment even if the payoff is years down the road.

As we've seen in the previous chapter, you can probably show your boss an ROI model where your cost to raise a bequest dollar is between three and five cents. We'll bet dollars to donuts that you don't have another fundraising method that raises so much for so little!

SECURING PAINLESS COMMITMENTS TO CONTINGENT INVESTMENT

It's January, and your organization is making its final budget decisions for a new fiscal year that will start on April 1. For the third year in a row, you've submitted a proposal for a legacy gift marketing investment – and for the third year in a row, the response comes back that *'we just don't have the money.'*

Here's another way to come at it. Leave next year's budget for everyone else to fight over, and go to a new battleground. Why not try a pitch like this?

> *"I'd like to propose that 20% of all bequest revenue we receive in the next five years be set aside for legacy marketing investments."*

If you're in a smaller to medium-sized organization, the odds are that you don't budget fully for expected legacy revenues. The strategy here is to go after unbudgeted revenues. Even though you don't know when they'll come in, maybe you'll get a commitment that you'll get a share when and if they do.

TELL STORIES THAT MAKE EVERYBODY FEEL GOOD

We've already learned that the most powerful persuader for legacy giving is the donor who has already made a legacy gift herself. When you find the right storyteller and you tell the story in all its passion and richness, you'll do more than influence your legacy prospects. You'll remind your leadership, staff, and stakeholders of why your mission matters, why yours is a noble cause, and why you're all so lucky to be working together to leave this world better than you found it.

We've seen it time and time again. A beautifully-told legacy story makes everyone feel great about their association with your organization – and each other. When you accomplish this, you're building a culture that values legacy giving and the shared legacy that each and every one of you is helping to create for the generations who will follow you.

ENLISTING A CHAMPION

We've all been in this position: We're staff fundraisers who have great ideas, a lot of knowledge, and a true vision of where our fundraising programs should be headed. But, no one seems to listen to us. No one takes us as seriously as we think they should. We don't know if this *'we don't listen to our staff fundraiser'* syndrome has a name, but we think it should – because it's endemic!

Sometimes the message isn't the issue – it's the messenger. And, like it or not, sometimes you, the staff fundraiser, are not the right messenger.

If there's one tipping point that can generate some much-needed momentum to your legacy giving program, it's having a passionate champion on your Board of Directors. If you can recruit and ignite just one person on your board, then she can evangelize to her peers in a way that you simply can't. For example, it's pretty hard for you to preach to your Board Members that they should all make legacy gifts. But, if you have a Board Member who has done it and implores everyone to leave even a small gift in their wills, your chances of increasing board involvement go way up. As all fundraisers know, the best fundraiser is the one who it's hardest to say no to!

SET CONFIDENT GOALS

Here's an example. Say Awesome Birding Canada raises about $1 million every year. Legacy giving accounts for 5%, or $50,000, of that revenue in an average year.

You come along and tell your leadership that there are charities in Canada who are generating legacy gifts worth more than 20% of total fundraised income – and that many in the UK achieve 30% or more.

You then lay out a plan that shows how you believe that you can increase your legacy gift revenue from 5% to 25%. Not only that, when your legacy revenues reach $250,000 per year, your organization will have achieved overall revenue growth of 20% – from $1 million to $1.2 million per year.

Then, ask your leadership how they would spend another $200,000 a year on programs, and sit back while the discussion ensues.

This is a situation that requires you to put yourself on the line and take a risk. That's what leaders and visionaries do. In our opinion, life is just too short to not go for the gusto!

HAVING A JOB DESCRIPTION THAT'S WRITTEN DOWN – SPECIFICALLY!

Here's another scenario we come across all the time: We get a call from a fundraiser who wants to talk about his legacy giving program. When we get started in the conversation, we ask how much of his time is dedicated to planned giving, as opposed to the other types of fundraising they're expected to do. After all, most planned giving fundraisers wear more than one hat! The answer is usually something like, *"Well, I'm supposed to spend 20% of my time on this, but in truth, I hardly do it at all."*

The hard truth is that while no one would argue the importance of legacy giving to a great fundraising program, few would argue that legacy giving is *urgent*. And, in our post-2008-market-meltdown world, urgency trumps important just about every time. We've stretched and squeezed so much out of the *'do more with less'* idea that many of us are running on fumes.

There has never been a more important time than now to have a serious conversation with your boss or human resource person – whoever does your annual performance review or whatever your equivalent is.

You need to get a written confirmation that you'll spend 10% or 20% (or whatever) of your time on legacy giving, and then you need to stick to that commitment. This can be unpleasant and difficult, as setting any kind of boundaries in any relationship can be. When you're pressed to help pull off the gala at the last minute, you may have to say no because you've got a legacy deadline to meet.

In our experience, it's critical for one person in any shop, no matter how small, to stick to their legacy guns until the money starts coming in. Once people see the revenue grow, the whole picture will change. Trust us on this one! But until that change happens, you need to be the lonely soul who remains committed to the consistent and disciplined pursuit of legacy gifts.

MAKING YOUR WINS *THEIR* WINS

In his book, *Leaders Eat Last,* author Simon Sinek talks about the unselfishness of military generals who wait until all the new recruits are fed before they get in line for breakfast in the mess hall. We love this principle of putting others' needs first – and we think it can be applied to legacy giving.

The partners at Good Works have always lived by the rule that they share the credit and take the blame. If a client is thrilled with a project, the partner spreads the praise to the whole team of Good Workers who were involved. But, if the client is unhappy over a mess-up, the partner single-handedly takes the blame. Our partners believe that sharing credit and taking blame is a central tenet of what makes our company – and every Good Worker – so special.

You can apply the same principle to your planned giving program. If a donor ever calls with a complaint – whether it's a misspelled name or an unwanted phone call – take the blame personally. Own it yourself and accept that these things happen once in a while.

But when a lawyer calls you and tells you that there's a bequest worth $232,000 on its way to your charity, drop everything and create a celebration! Run around the office and hug people. Use the word 'we' a lot – like *"look what we did!*" Make everyone feel like they were a part of making that gift happen.

The trick of it all is simple: If your colleagues, stakeholders, leaders, volunteers (or whoever) feel good about getting that bequest, they'll want to have that feeling again. And they'll start doing things that they think will help that feeling come back. If you behave like this often enough, you'll have established a legacy giving culture at your shop – and you'll make a lot of money down the road because of it.

CREATE A POOL OF SNEEZERS AND STORYTELLERS

Nothing encourages your leaders and co-workers to get enthused about legacy giving more than hearing raves from your legacy donors. After all, when your bequesters praise your organization, your leaders and teammates feel like they're being praised as well.

If you get a notification from a donor that you're in her will, we encourage you to drop everything and give her a call!

Invite her to tell you the story of how she first discovered you, how she started supporting you and how she decided to make her bequest. (Sidenote: don't do this on the first call! Get to know her first to avoid feeling slimy). Once she's shared her story, impress upon her how wonderful her story is, and how it could inspire others to make a gift in their will too. Whether she agrees to give you a short testimonial-style quote for your newsletter or she agrees to be the signatory for a letter or to make a video, impress on her that her story has the power to raise hundreds of thousands of dollars to forward your mission and advance your cause.

As we've already said, donor stories are incredibly powerful tools you can use to persuade your prospects to make bequests. But, they're also powerful at making your leaders and colleagues feel good about your legacy program. And, when your Board Members hear endorsements like this from your donors, they'll be more likely to approve your legacy gift marketing budget next year!

WINNING THE OFFICE POLITICS GAME

The key to being successful within your organization is to be strategic, to be disciplined, and to be patient. Come up with an internal persuasion game plan and then stick to it religiously. Don't be frustrated if it doesn't work right away. They'll see the light in their own good time — and then you can *really* get to work!

CHAPTER 11:
FINAL THOUGHTS

Over the years, we've developed a bit of a fascination with how people live, how people age and prepare for death, and as they make that journey, what really matters as we take our final breaths.

We've soaked up information on the well-lived life from all sorts of sources. We've read articles and books. We've listened to conference speakers and TED talks. When you get right down to it, we're existential junkies!

From all of our learning, we can summarize the three most important elements of a well-lived life. When people in their nineties say they're content with how their lives have gone, they pretty much touch on the same three ideas:

PEOPLE NEED PURPOSE
Do you remember Victor Frankl's book *Man's Search for Meaning* from Chapter 5? Academics from all sorts of disciplines agree that we humans are hardwired for

purpose and meaning. We need to have something to do that matters – and when it matters to somebody else as well as us, so much the better.

For some reason, many of us love the idea of continuing to live out our purpose even after we're gone. When we have purpose, we matter. When we can make a positive difference in someone else's life, we feel noble and needed.

Unhappy older people will sometimes tell you that they've lost their purpose. That their lives have lost their meaning. This is common when some people retire from their career, or lose their driver's license for medical reasons as they get older.

Happy older people still have great reasons to get up in the morning and to do something that matters, to them and often to others. In fact, as we age, we appreciate that our time is limited and we savour our usefulness even more.

So, when you talk with your legacy prospects and donors about their bequests, make sure you talk explicitly about the purpose and meaning inherent in these gifts. That kind of language will resonate with each one's higher self.

WE NEED TO BELONG

For millions of years, we humans have been evolving into the most social of all species on earth.

Few things are as painful to a human being as being shunned, ostracized, or isolated. Think of the child being punished by being sent to his room alone. We all have a very primal hunger for contact. For conversation. For connection. For storytelling. For approval and acceptance.

You can frame legacy gifts as an opportunity for your supporter to belong to a truly wonderful group of people – a group that has committed its love to the generation that will follow. And, depending on your cause, you can probably frame the beneficiary of the legacy gift as becoming more connected and achieving a greater sense of belonging as well.

This can be beautiful stuff if you take the time to express it in all its humanity.

ALL YOU NEED IS LOVE

John Lennon said it best. The last (and most important!) of the three things that make for a well-lived life is simple. Lots and lots of love. Giving it. Receiving it. Sharing it.

Every fundraiser knows that the word *philanthropy* comes from the Greek for *love of humankind*. The magic of legacy gift fundraising is that it's the one place where most everyday, middle-class people have the chance to transcend from being 'just donors' to 'philanthropists'.

Think of Jacqueline, who you met in the introduction to this book. Now, she has made many, many charitable donations in her life – but rarely were any of them for more than $100. But, when Jacqueline leaves 10% of her estate to the Canadian Cancer Society, her gift will be a little over $100,000. That's a lot of love – and it should be talked about that way.

At the end of the day, legacy giving isn't about money. And, it isn't about death.

Legacy giving is about life. And purpose. And belonging. And love – lots and lots of love.

REFERENCES

*Collectively, we've done a lot reading over the past 15-20 years. While we've tried to cite throughout the book and compile a comprehensive list of references, we likely have missed books and articles that should appear here.

Crawford, Rachel and Hartwick, Fred. 2001. Creating and Maintaining A Planned Giving Society. Journal of Gift Planning, 5(4), pp. 19-52.

DameGreene, Susan. 2003. How to Develop a Successful Bequest Program: A Simple, Easy-to-Follow Plan for Starting, Increasing and Collecting Bequests At Your Nonprofit. The Journal of Gift Planning, 7(2), pp. 17-52.

Erikson, Erik. 1950. Childhood and Society. New York: WW Norton

Erikson, Erik. 1959. Identity and the Lifecycle. New York. WW Norton.

Fonda, Jane. Life's Third Act. 2011. TedX Women. Available at: https://www.ted.com/talks/jane_fonda_life_s_third_act

Frankl, Victor. 2006. Man's Search for Meaning. Boston: Beacon Press.

Gauthier, Bernard. 2018. Strategic Communication in Canada: Planning Effective PR Campaigns. Toronto: Canadian Scholars' Press Inc.

Gilmartin, Jim. 2015. Do You Have A Story To Tell? Baby Boomers Want To Hear It. MediaPost. Available at: https://www.mediapost.com/publications/article/247160/do-you-have-a-story-to-tell-baby-boomers-want-to.html

Green, Fraser, VanHerpt, Jose, and McDonald, Beth. 2007. Iceberg Philanthropy: Unlocking Extraordinary Gifts from Ordinary Donors. Ottawa: BookSurge Publishing.

Green, Fraser. 2010. State of the Legacy Nation. Ottawa: Good Works Communications.

Green, Fraser. 2014. State of the Legacy Nation. Ottawa: Good Works Communications. Available at: http://think.goodworksco.ca/state-of-legacy-nation

Green, Fraser. 2019. State of the Legacy Nation. Ottawa: Good Works Communications. Available at: https://think.goodworksco.ca/state-of-legacy-nation-2019

James, Russell. 2013. Inside the Mind of the Bequest Donor: A visual presentation of the neuroscience and psychology of effective planned giving communication. Texas: CreateSpace Independent Publishing Platform.

James, Russell. 2014. Myths in Planned Giving: New Research Results. Available at: https://www.slideshare.net/rnja8c/myths-in-planned-giving-new-research-results. Slides 3-9.

James, Russell and O'Boyle, Michael. 2014. Charitable Estate Planning as Visualized Autobiography: An fMRI Study of Its Neural Correlates. Nonprofit and Voluntary Sector Quarterly, 43(2), pp. 355-373.

Lombrozo, Tania. 2013. The Truth About The Left Brain / Right Brain Relationship. National Public Radio. Available at: https://www.npr.org/sections/13.7/2013/12/02/248089436/the-truth-about-the-left-brain-right-brain-relationship

MacLean, Paul. 1990. The Triune Brain in Evolution: Role in Paleocerebral Functions. New York: Springer.

Maslow, Abraham. 1943. A Theory of Human Motivation. Psychological Review. 50(4), pp 370–96.

Plutchik, Robert. 1980. Emotion: Theory, research, and experience: Vol. 1. *Theories of emotion*. New York: Academic.

Ries, Jack and Trou, Al. 2001. Positioning: The Battle for the Mind. New York: McGraw-Hill Education.

Rosenbaum, Ernest, Chittenden, Eva, Hawgood, Jane, Joseph, Denah, von Ehrenkrook, Alexandra, Shapiro, Stephanie and Spiegel, David. 2019. Symbolic Immortality: Thoughts About the Future. California: Stanford Medicine. Available at: https://med.stanford.edu/survivingcancer/storytelling/symbolic-immortality-.html

Routely, Claire, Sargeant, Adrian and Day, Harriet. 2018. Everything Research Can Tell Us About Legacy Giving in 2018: A Literature Review. University of Plymouth: Hartsook Centre for Sustainable Philanthropy, commissioned by Legacy Voice. Available at: http://legacyvoice.co.uk/wp-content/uploads/2018/05/Legacy-Voice-lit-review_full-report_03.pdf

Sinek, Simon. 2014. Leaders Eat Last: Why Some Teams Pull Together and Others Don't. London: Portfolio.

Swank, Katherine. 2015. 24 Planned Giving Terms You Should Know. Charleston, SC: Blackbaud. Available at: https://www.blackbaud.com/files/resources/downloads/whitepaper_23plannedgivingtermsyoushouldknow.pdf

ABOUT THE AUTHORS

Fraser Green
Boomer

When Fraser Green joined Good Works in 1996, he wondered why there was such a huge gap between direct mail fundraising and planned giving. He thought instinctively that direct mail donors (who are older as a rule) should make great legacy prospects. Fraser spearheaded a poll of North American direct mail donors in 2003, that showed without question that direct mail donors have huge legacy giving potential – and that opened the floodgates. For almost 20 years now, Fraser has been writing books and blogs, speaking at conferences and working with charities all over North America – constantly searching for the perfect way to persuade everyday donors to make extraordinary gifts.

Holly Wagg
Gen X

By the time she was 40, Holly Wagg had already written her will 4 times – with the adoption of her first two children, the birth of her third child, when her wife was diagnosed with leukemia and when she became a widow. It will be re-written a 5th time when she remarries this year. It wasn't until she joined the Good Works team in 2012 that she was able to have her first substantial foray into planned giving as a fundraising professional. She began testing, tweaking, building upon and adding new elements to the Iceberg Philanthropy legacy giving model as imagined by Fraser Green. This book combines her legacy giving expertise with her lived experience to help you establish and execute a thoughtful and effective donor-centred program.

Charlotte Field
Millennial

A true digital native, Charlotte is always looking for ways to integrate offline and online channels into one seamless journey. So when she joined the Good Works team back in 2015, she immediately saw the opportunity to weave digital tactics into a best-practice legacy marketing program. Whether it's crafting email automations, developing donor-centric web copy, or building remarketing campaigns, she's seen how the right digital touchpoint can take a legacy campaign to the next level – and she's constantly looking for the next tool to best connect a donor with a cause they love.

ABOUT GOOD WORKS

Since 1986, Good Workers have been telling powerful philanthropic stories through direct response channels. We have always believed that it's relationships more than transactions that drive the bottom line in the long run — and that donor loyalty is the real key to fundraising success.

Good Works has leveraged its storytelling and direct response expertise to generate extraordinary legacy gifts from everyday annual donors. The multichannel legacy programs we create with our clients are built to last — and will be generating revenue for decades to come.

We believe that philanthropy is one of the highest and noblest forms of human expression. Our goal is to help everyday people to become their most loving and generous selves.

Learn more at www.goodworksco.ca.

Made in the USA
Middletown, DE
21 September 2019